I0004833

Bitcoin & Cryptocurrencies Guide

Introduction to Learning Everything You Need to Know!

Table of Contents

Introduction

The world of digital currency and how to trade and earn bitcoins can be confusing. This book is written in a way that will educate the reader and give them the information to make educated choices. It does not profess to make you a fortune in the new crypto currencies but, quite the opposite, it will arm you with the tools to enter the digital arena safely and knowledgeably.

The field of mining for bitcoin is explained in simple to follow terms, all the equipment you will need, the fees involved and the actual chances that you will be successful are laid out ready to be weighed up.

We will examine the means we have for analyzing the markets and the trends that are so important to spot if you are considering trading in digital currency. The volatility of the currency is explained and also the positive influences that can affect the price of bitcoin are considered carefully.

By understanding blockchain and the technological complexity of the protocol behind cryptocurrency, you can begin to appreciate the alternative uses for this revolutionary hardware and the way it is set to change society forever!

Does this worry the powers that be?? You bet it does. We look at the ways the currency terrifies government and shows us a future where the fate of our money will be in our hands only and not those of a third party.

Chapter 1: Blockchain, Bitcoin and Cryptocurrency Defined

2008 was a troubled time. The Occupy Wall Street movement was at its strongest. Accusations of misusing clients' money, misleading customers and charging hefty fees to do so were being leveled at major banks and other financial institutions. Pioneers of the new age of crypto currency saw a chance to put the seller in charge of his own money. By cutting out the middleman, they saw a way to make all transactions more transparent and eliminate interest fees and create a corruption free environment for all sellers.

By creating decentralized system two entities can trade directly with each other and know exactly what is happening with their funds.

By examining the properties of bitcoin, we can begin to understand how innovative this new currency really is. Prior to 2008, the idea of an alternative currency was unheard of, since its original concept, bitcoin has progressed at a pace that is impressive to say the least.

1. **Secure**: All funds are locked securely in a cryptography system that can only be accessed by a public key. The length of this number coupled with strong cryptography means that the chance of hacking or duplication is nonexistent. Your bitcoin address is as secure as Area 51!

2. **Irreversible**: Nobody, and I mean nobody, can reverse a transaction. Once confirmed there is no way back. If you send money and confirm the transaction, then it has been paid and there is no reversing the process. Unfortunately, if you have sent funds to a source that is not completely

legitimate, there is no safety net. As with other purchases, it is recommended that all transactions are examined thoroughly.

3. **Global and speedy:** Due to the nature of the processing of bitcoins your actual physical location and that of the recipient are irrelevant. All trades are carried out by a network of computers and are therefore confirmed in minutes.

4. **Anonymous**: Bitcoins are connected to accounts and addresses not people. Trades are conducted between accounts that are symbolized purely by chains of characters that are up to 30 symbols long. No identities are attached to these chains so while it is possible to follow the flow of the transaction, it is completely free from attachment to details of the parties involved.

5. **Restriction free:** Who do you need to ask for permission to use bitcoin? No one at all! It is software that can be used for free by anyone anywhere. The lack of restriction and hierarchy is one of the properties of the new crypto currencies that appeals the most. By creating a new currency that is available to a set of people who may not have been allowed access to standard methods of banking and trading, it is paving the way for huge changes in society.

Bitcoin is free from government interference and is completely transparent. International trades can take place without involving exchange rates and the charges that accompanies them. The mathematical framework that supports the crypto currency system is unaffected by political pressure and human error. It is hard to see how the future cannot be changed by the emergence of this new era of banking and trading and it has been said that bitcoin is to banks what email was to the postal industry.

Blockchain is the technology behind bitcoin and is being hailed as one of the greatest innovations of modern times. The technology allows both parties in a transaction to connect directly and removes the need for a third party.

The customer wishes to send money to the supplier, this is the transaction and details of the trade are now represented online in the form of a block.

1. The block is now broadcast to all parties in the network. Once approved the transaction is deemed valid.
2. The block that was created to represent this trade is now added to the chain and is used to record a permanent and transparent record.
3. The money agreed upon now moves from customer to supplier.

Blockchain is not only the technology that can allow the march forward of crypto currency, but it is also holds the potential to transform business, government and society as a whole. Intrigued?? Let's examine how this new technological genie can affect human affairs for the better.

We are all aware of the Internet and how it has improved communication and collaboration. However it has done little to change how we conduct business. Intermediaries are needed to govern how we conduct transactions and exchanges of value. This generates fees, a fact we have all accepted in the past and paid, albeit grudgingly. However, the emergence of blockchain that allows data trading between billions of devices without a third-party involvement.

The Internet of everything is a term that is being used more freely as the digital age marches on but the emergence of blockchain means that we can create a ledger of everything! Imagine every smart device in use connecting and sharing information and trading freely with each other.

Every transaction and exchange of data will be recorded, indelibly and transparently. By acting as a ledger of all accounts it becomes the worlds database, societies notary and clearing house. The protocol of blockchain is what establishes the rules. Trust is hard coded into the platform that governs blockchain and ensues the integrity of all the data that is traded amongst the billions of devices that will use it.

Chapter 2: How Value is Traded and the Risks Involved

Bitcoin trading is a new and highly exciting opportunity for both professionals and beginners. It is a new market, prone to highly fragmented and massive spreads. Cryptocurrency is appealing to new investors because its short history is littered with peaks and troughs.

Every time bitcoin has a "bubble "and increases in value, the media attention is such that interest is spiked and the value increases even more. Trading bitcoin is simple and global and provides an opportunity for investing to a whole new class of investors and speculators.

Before we explore how to trade bitcoin we must first understand why it appeals to people. Below are a few points about crypto currency trading that make it exciting and unique.

- **Bitcoin trades 24/7**

  Standard stock markets open and close based on geographical location but as BTC is global and uses exchanges instead of markets it can be traded at any time. There is no official bitcoin exchange, which means there is no official price attached to the currency. Generally, most exchanges stay within the same range of value and this can lead to arbitrage opportunities which appeals to some traders.

Bitcoin is volatile

News events, statements by governments and other geopolitical factors can affect the value of cryptocurrencies. When the bankruptcy of Mt. Gox was reported in 2014 it appeared in headlines worldwide and drove the value of the currency down rapidly.

Similarly, the association with Silk Road and the negative press that followed impacted upon the value and saw huge drops in price.

It was subsequently argued by crypto friendly investors that this was a sign that the market was maturing and saw the price recover in the weeks that followed both news events.

- **Bitcoin is not a fiat currency**

While the value of bitcoin is affected by world events, it has the benefit of existing outside the influence of any single country or economy. Standard currencies are directly related to the country or economy that governs it. However, cryptocurrencies are unique in their global pricing.

Now we have established the reasons for trading in bitcoin we need to explore how we choose an exchange as there is no official bitcoin exchange. A number of factors have to be taken into account when selecting which exchange is the best for your personal experience.

1. Location: If your first deposit is going to be in a fiat currency you must ensure that the exchange you choose accepts the currency you will be using.
2. Charges: Examine the fees that will be generated by your trade and compare with other exchanges. As this is relatively new field major differences in rates can be found across the board.
3. Liquidity: Depending on the volume of your trade you may need to explore the market depth of your chosen exchange. Large traders will need to ensure the liquidity of their chosen partner.

Taking into account these factors we can examine the exchanges that are currently dominating the market.

- **Coinbase**

  The first regulated exchange in the US Coinbase is a digital asset exchange, located in San Francisco it trades in bitcoin, Ethereum and lite coin and accepts fiat currencies from 32 different countries.

- **Bitstamp**

  Founded in 2011 it is one of the oldest exchanges dealing with bitcoin. Based in Luxembourg it trades USD for cryptocurrency and allows USD, EUR and bitcoin withdrawals and deposits.

- **Kraken**

  Currently the #1 exchange in EUR trading it is also a top 15 exchange when looking at USD volume. It has also considered to be the most secure exchange as its system has never been breached by hackers.

Now we will use one of the exchanges above to explain how to trade bitcoin for the first time. We will use Kraken as the example, but the process is generally governed by the same principles across all exchanges.

Firstly, create an account by tapping the black box in the corner that indicates the sign-up process. You will receive an email that will allow you to confirm your account, once this is done you are required to log in and confirm all your personal information.

All bitcoin exchanges require differing levels of verification by law. The standard level of information means that you will have to supply your full name, date of birth, country of residence and phone number. Some exchanges may require further verification of your address.

Once you have followed these steps you will need to navigate to the "funding" tab. A screen will appear that will contain a selection of funding methods. Kraken offers many different options for your deposit including:

- EUR Bank wire deposit: minimum $5 and only available in EEA countries

- USD Bank wire deposit: $5 fee and only available in the US

- JPY Bank deposit: no fees but there is a minimum of 5.000-yen deposit and available in Japan only

- GBP SEPA and swift deposit: 10 pounds minimum and 19% fee

Deposits made involving the traditional banking methods will take up to three days to clear where as BTC requires six different confirmations and will be cleared in around an hour.

Now navigate to the trade tab and by utilizing the black bar across the top of the page you can switch pairs for trading. Block A will display the amount of money in your account.

Block B will display the fee you will pay for the exchange.

Block C is where you can select the amount of coins you would like to purchase or how much money you wish to spend on your transaction.

Block D is the preferred price, default settings means the price available is set by the last deal.

Once you press the "submit" button your order will be processed and the coins will appear in your account literally minutes after you have pressed the tab.

We now know how to trade in bitcoin and use the exchanges to obtain cryptocurrency by exchanging our traditional monies for bitcoins.

We also need to be aware of the ever-growing ways we can obtain cryptocurrencies for, as demand increases, so do opportunities to purchase. E-Bay currently offer chances to buy the different currencies and other auction sites are cottoning on to the idea. By checking out local bitcoin opportunities in your area via Google or another search engine you can discover local bitcoin sellers and buyers and arrange to meet and trade coins.

Extra caution must be observed when dealing offline, only meet during daytime hours and make sure you are accompanied by a friend. Common sense precautions need to prevail when you are not shielded by the anonymity of the web!

As with all trading, there are a number of risks that need to be addressed and considered. Cryptocurrency is different from other currencies as it is regarded as a commodity. This has never been the case with traditional money and means that digital coinage are subject to market fluctuations as with any other commodity or stock.

Considering the age of this young and active commodity it can mean that the markets will dip and rise wildly. When investing in bitcoin it is generally a rule of thumb to take a "big picture" stance and refuse to be panicked by a drop in value.

Digital currency is encrypted to make them secure and here we can discover a potential failing with the commodity. The coding is designed to identify the actual currency but not the owner, hence the anonymity we have already covered. Nothing within the specifics identify the currency as yours, meaning that if it is taken fraudulently then it is gone! You have no recourse to reclaim what is yours.

Worst case scenario, cryptocurrency could, in theory, become worthless. Visit the bitcoin site and in amongst the FAQ there is an admission that should the investors interest wane to such an extent that overall effect on world economy could affect the value of the digital currency so severely that it loses all value! As in other situations we encounter no matter how effective safeguards are extreme factors can lead to extreme reactions.

These comments are not meant to put you off your foray into cryptocurrency just arm you with facts that will enable you to view the experience with a level of knowledge you did not have formerly.

Chapter 3: How Values Fluctuate and How the Currency Attains Value

Bitcoin presents opportunities that were unheard of prior to its development. Never before has a currency had the same properties as a commodity. Given the relative newness and the unique status of the currency it is only to be expected that a great deal of uncertainty will accompany all aspects of the usage and trading that accompany it.

Normally stock and its level of volatility are measured on traditional markets using a volatility index or VIX. Crypto currency is classed as an asset class and as it is still in a fledgling stage and as such bitcoin is yet to have a generally accepted index and therefore there is no clear indication of the levels of inconstancy achieved by bitcoin.

There are many factors that impact this volatility and below we will address a few of these factors.

The media effect: The majority of people will remember their first encounter with the world of cryptocurrency most probably occurred around the same time as they heard about the dark web and, more importantly, Silk Road and the nefarious activities that were reportedly occurring. Hailed as the currency that allowed drug dealers, arms merchants and even "hitman to play their wares anonymously it was not a good time for bitcoin.

The arrest and trial of Ross Ulbricht made sure that Silk Road received a massive amount of media coverage. He was indicted on charges of conspiring to traffic narcotics, hacking, laundering funds and even attempting to have six people killed.

The trial was big news from 13th of January 2013 until the 4th of February 2013 when Ulbricht was convicted.
During the closure of Silk Road, it is reported that the FBI seized a huge amount of bitcoins and plans were made to liquidate the assets after the trial. The 27th of June 2014 saw the US Marshal Service sell a large number of bitcoins in an online auction.

The whole Silk Road experience did nothing to improve the image of bitcoin as an alternative to traditional currency but what it did do was to increase public awareness. So, the period following the closure of the online market saw a sharp drop in value, however the accompanying level of awareness meant that a whole new class of buyers that could look past the negative media coverage. This then lead to a sharp increase in price a short time later.

Option value: There is very little option value to investors who hold a whole load of currency. Due to the nature of the market investors who hold over $10 million do not have a clear indication what would happen if they decided to liquidate their stock. By moving their cryptocurrency into the fiat market, they would severely affect the market. This fact means that bitcoin is viewed as a small cap stock and as such cannot achieve the levels of stability that other options on the market are able to.

Security: Investors react to news of security breaches and in order to produce a more stable source, it is imperative that the community behind bitcoin exposes all security vulnerabilities in order to achieve solutions.

This approach to security is a great way to produce the best outcomes, but by putting their concerns in the public domain they can panic the market and cause massive drops in price. The whole fundamental premise that allows full and frank examination of all aspects of the software and encourages user input regarding the developments of source code is part of the reason the levels of price are so robust for BTC. The downside of this protocol design is that there will be security breaches and they will be widely reported and cause volatility in price.

Tax: When the IRS announced a statement that it now regards BTC as an asset for tax purposes it had a mixed effect on the price of the currency. The downside to the new status of the cryptocurrency meant that there was a new level of complexity when using BTC for purchases.

However small the transaction the market value of the currency would have to be recorded. Understandably this has slowed rates of adoption as the new tax laws make it a lot more difficult to use the currency and it can be seen as too much bother. Another downside of this statement from the IRS is the indication that more regulations are bound to follow. To achieve the level of adoption that is required to confirm its overall utilization in society the currency will need to be free of strong regulations. This pointer from the IRS could mean a slowing of adoption that could be incredibly damaging for the BTC.
There is however an upside to the new tax treatment. Recognition of the currency, in any form, tends to boost the market and increase valuation.

Next, we will address the different factors that lead to the currency attaining value.

Media interest: As in volatility the media plays a huge part in bringing virtual currency to the attention of the masses. Social media has played a massive part in increasing the value of the crypto currency. Intrinsically the value of bitcoin derives from our vision of how it will emerge from the depths of the internet and impact on our lives.

Social media provided an early breeding ground for bitcoin in the early days, often discussed on forums and mailing lists the online meetings were often people's first inkling that digital money was a concept that was coming. The people who were hearing about BTC and getting excited about its potential future were the people who were conducting online transactions and therefore establishing value.

Today the effect of social media on the market value of the digital currency cannot be ignored. Positive stories about new technology or breakthrough innovations are spread like wildfire and even lead to endorsements from high profile figures in the media.

Many times, such endorsements can strengthen the public's perception and increase activity on the exchanges that will lead to an increase in value. Coupled with blockchain based platforms that are actually using BTC to reward their users for spreading information about the currency and drumming up new interest it would seem that the crypto currency is well aware of the attention economy and how it can impact on value.

Global adoption: Currently bitcoin is seen to reside and thrive in developed, wealthy and tech savvy countries but with the problems of inflation, fraud, accessibility and exchange growing daily it would be foolish to ignore the possibilities that global adoption of the currency could bring. China and Japan have already impacted heavily on the value of bitcoin and with Japan seemingly ready to make moves that will see a rise in use within its own economy it can only lead to further rises in value.

Japan seems to have a completely different attitude to digital currency than some other countries. It seems to be displaying an amount of trust and interest in the currency that it cannot fail to impact the price. Confidence is high in Japan and the rest of the countries that are currently not involved with BTC are watching closely.

It does not necessarily follow that other developed countries will follow in suit soon, it is a massive boost to the status of the digital currency.
Considering the checkered past that Japan has with the cryptocurrency it is seen as a huge endorsement for the currency to allow bitcoin as a valid currency and also the passing of a law that states bitcoin users will not be taxed directly. Since the Mt. Gox incident occurred in Tokyo and has affected Japan and its relationship with BTC in a positive way, regulations are in place that will protect customers and prevent another disaster. Rather than letting Mt Gox cloud the perception of digital currencies it has been used positively and lessons have been learnt.

- Retail: Without people using bitcoin on a day to day basis it has no worth as a currency. The very nature of currency means that it has to be used regularly. With each major retail company that accepts digital currency the appeal of the crypto coin is growing,
Some of the biggest companies in the world accept bitcoin and we can take a look at how they have incorporated the coin in their business practices,

- **Virgin Galactic**: It is well documented that Richard Branson is one of the leading advocates of blockchain, the technology behind bit coin. In the past, he has been very vocal about the differences that blockchain can make to society overall. By accepting bitcoin as payment for his much-publicized space exploration program he has put the weight of the Virgin name behind the coin. This can only lead to further confidence in the currency and this will reflect in the market.

- **WordPress**: This popular blogging platform at first sight may not seem a major player but when it is taken into consideration for its users a different picture appears. CNN, NBC, The New York Times and Reuters are amongst the biggest media companies in the world and they all use WordPress. By accepting BTC WordPress has endorsed the currency and so, it would seem, have some of its powerful users.

- **Tesla**: Proving that regular bricks and mortar businesses are also accepting digital currency it was reported that a Lamborghini showroom located in California had just sold a $100,000-dollar Tesla and used bitcoin to seal the purchase. This was quickly followed by the second sale from the same dealership using the crypto currency. The more companies that begin to accept the currency will mean that the opportunities to support the whole system will flourish

- **Pizza for Coins**: From Virgin Galactic to the humble pizza delivery company the message is clear, we are going to allow our customers to use BTC to buy stuff!! This service allows customers to order Domino's pizza using the digital coin. Simply send your name and address to the company, they will send you the online menu. Order your food, pay with your bitcoin and within ten minutes pizza for coins will verify your payment and order your food.

- **Overstock.com**: The biggest retailer to accept bitcoin the company has been supporting the currency since Jan 2013

With every new company that gets behind bitcoin the confidence in the currency grows, this is then reflected in the market price. Major public figures such as Richard Branson are firmly behind the currency. Let's take a look at some celebrities and see comments that they made in regards bitcoin.

- **Lily Allen**: reportedly the singer was asked to do a gig and receive payment in bitcoins and she declined. In a tweet in 2014 she proclaimed herself to be a #idiot #idiot!

- **Mel B**: the former Spice Girl partnered with Cloud Hashing to become the first ever artist to accept BTC for her music. She used the service in a bid to "join together fans across the world"

- **Roseanne Barr**: The actress/comedian who is well known for her involvement in political movements urged her Twitter followers to educate themselves on the digital currency and support the innovative new currency.

- **Snoop Dogg**: In a facetious tweet, the controversial rapper announced his next album would be "available in bitcoin" and "delivered by drone" and although his remarks were meant to be taken lightly the waves of attention brought to the currency by the public was off the scale.

Chapter 4: How to Identify Trends in Bitcoin Price Charts

Traders often make decisions based on basic falls and rises in a market, often relying on instinct to determine when to buy and sell there has to be a better way to make such important decisions. Trends are an important source of information that will allow traders to identify patterns in price data and act accordingly.

When you study a bitcoin price chart it is hard to ignore the fact that prices seem to follow invisible lines. This fact is applicable when looking at charts based on any timeline. Studying a chart based on hourly movement compared to a chart that maps weekly movement the same lines can be spotted.

These lines are called "trend lines" and it is important to understand how to read them and interpret the trends they are identifying. Of course, if it was that simple then everybody would be getting rich investing in BTC so we need to delve deeper in order to use this important data to aid investment.

It quickly becomes apparent that the charts show two trend lines, an upper trend and a lower trend, prices will fluctuate between the two. Known as a trend channel this is one of the most widely used concepts when studying technical price analysis. It is important to understand how to read these trends and then divide them into shorter segments and then again to shorten these segments to glean the most information.

It is essential to recognize the fractal nature of the data and accept that they will appear to be very similar no matter what time frame is used.

It is not difficult to draw trend lines, simply arm yourself with a charting platform such as Bitcoin Charts or Zero Block that will allow you to interactively draw on charts. Within these platforms you will find "line" or "channel" tools and now we will learn how to use them.

Firstly, we will chart the uptrend of a chart. Generally, uptrends are used to represent the lower supporting trend line in a more accurate fashion so in order to map this trend the line will start at one of the low points of the trend and will extend to one of the next higher lows. The tool that you are using will then automatically veer to the left and/or right.

It is important to note that the line will almost always need adjustment, by moving the line so that it incorporates the trends price lows as accurately as is possible you will achieve an indication of the trends identified. It is worth noting that trend lines will never fit prices without some flaws but when used correctly it should be possible to identify some salient price information which can aid your trading decisions.

In order to create the trend channel a downtrend line will need to be charted, this is done in exactly the same way as the uptrend line, starting with the upper resisting trend line. A down trend line is created by joining all declining peaks.

It is worth pointing out that it is impossible to create trend lines with only one peak on a chart. There needs to be multiple peaks in order to create a meaningful trend line.

It is important to be able to identify trends and know when they reverse. Technical analysis is all about identifying trends in the market and riding them until they reverse.

When trading on the cryptocurrency market the more tools you have in your armory the better. Understanding technical analysis relies on a comprehensive knowledge of the Dow Theory on which the analysis is based.

1. When pricing BTC or other cryptocurrencies the market considers everything. Asset prices are based on existing, prior and upcoming details. When applied to bitcoin and other currencies these have specific variables. Any regulations that are put into place that affect any part of the currency will affect the prices. Current demand is equally as important as past and future demands. The price of coins at any time is a representation of all details available, expectations are considered alongside tangible facts when pricing stock. The technicians that interpret these considerations are key to the pricing structure that is so important to traders and investors.

2. Technicians are less interested in variables and more focused on price. Even though the variables are what govern the price there are too many different aspects to be studied individually. Ultimately price is what governs trends and trends are how the traders make profit. Supply and demand of the product is a main staple in determining price and as the supply of BTC is widely known and has a transparency that is inapplicable to fiat currencies.
   a. Generally speaking the supply of BTC are along the following lines, laid down by protocol created at the inception of BTC.

- Every 15 mins or so a miner or group of miners will uncover a block of BTC that is their reward for solving problems and puzzles.
- Known as the block reward its initial value was 50BTC but has been halved every 4 years since then.
- The final quantity of BTC will be achieved in 2140 but because of the structure of the protocol it is a simple task to track supply.

3. Price movements aren't arbitrary. It is all about trends and trends are formed by the coins themselves. Once established it will generally follow the trend than oppose it. It is the task of technical analysts to predict the length of the upward trends and use this knowledge to profit from trading.

4. Past trends will tend to get repeated. One way to get a jump on the market is by recognizing a set of stimuli that has prompted an uptrend in the past and be aware of a similar set of catalysts that will prompt the same movement. Market psychology does have a measure of predictability about it, often trader's reaction can be predicted by using these methods.

We have identified trend lines and how to create them, we have learnt what their significance to the markets are, now we will explore the horizontal lines that can be tracked on a bitcoin price chart.

These horizontal lines are used to express varying levels of resistance and support. Determining these levels helps us to draw informed conclusions regarding the current supply and demand of the coin. For instance, if a substantial number of traders are seemingly willing to buy the currency at any one time and thus creates a large demand.

This can indicate that the price of the BTC is considered low and has created a demand for the stock. Once the premium price is close a "floor" of buyers is created.

The existence of such a large demand can often halt a decline and if strong enough can even turn a decline into an upward trend and increase in price.

Resistance levels are an exact opposite. Sellers will be sitting on their stock and waiting for an upward trend. By forming a large supply zone, a "ceiling" price is created and whenever the price of BTC approaches this level it is hindered by these supply stacks and forced to retreat.

Lateral movement can be identified and this can lead to trade-offs between support and resistance levels. By gathering around support lines and promoting sales around resistance levels the trade-off situation can be achieved.

We must be aware that false breakouts can occur that will fail to affect the trend and in order to identify a viable trend we must take note of trading volumes.

Trading volume is a major factor when identifying trends and their validity. A strong movement in price will be represented by a high volume of trade. Low trading volumes will accompany weak trends and lower prices. When a drop in price is evident it is advisable to check the accompanying volume achieved during the decline. There are two differing volumes and a long-term trend of growth will be represented by a rising volume of increases and a lower volume of declines.

By monitoring the volumes, we can identify when an upward trend is coming to an end as the volume will decrease during increases. The change in a downward trend will similarly be indicated by volume increase during decreases.

Moving averages is another tool used by technical analyzers and is another factor in simplifying trend recognition. To calculate the moving average a coin's price will be charted over a certain period of time. For example, to calculate the moving average on a certain date the price of the coin will be charted for the previous twenty days and will be calculated to obtain the moving average. When a number of moving averages have been calculated they can then be connected to form lines and indicate a pattern.

By creating a varied number of moving averages and the lines they create it can indicate a positive trend on the horizon. If a 20-day moving average crosses a 5-day moving average on a bitcoin pricing chart this could be a pointer that traders can use to invest wisely.

We have established a number of ways that technical analysis can assist traders and identify trends. Market sentiment is analyzed and along with all data that is available traders can invest wisely and hopefully, profitably.

We now have the knowledge of the technical side of trading but we must be aware of the pitfalls. Below we will find a number of tips to help avoid mistakes.

- Recognize that trading is a zero-sum game that is for everyone making a profit there is someone who is taking a loss. The whole crypto currency market is waiting for beginners to make mistakes, so never trade without full knowledge of your strategy during the trade and afterwards. Never trade just because you promised yourself you would trade daily, sometimes it is better to just sit on your coins and wait for better opportunities.

- Recognize FOMO that is the fear of missing out!! We are aware of the volatility of the crypto market and often it can be too easy to get swept up in a huge price hike of a certain coin and it can be hard to walk away. Once you have mastered the art of patience and you have learnt not to take notice of hype and lame people jumping on a bandwagon you will be able to keep moving forward.

- Understand risk management. In order to become a profitable trader, you will learn to avoid peaks of movements. You will benefit from small profits that will eventually turn these into a profit that is considerable.

- Volatility: Bitcoin is a volatile asset when related to fiat currencies but it is a lesser known fact that bitcoin activities have an inverse relationship with Altcoins. If the value of bit coins is rising then the value of Altcoins is falling and when the value of Altcoin is high, bitcoin prices will fall. It is important to have this level of knowledge before trading as the obvious pitfalls become apparent immediately.

- Fees: Bear in mind that multiple trades will incur multiple fees, explore the different fees available and factor this in when you are choosing the exchange that you will trade on.

Remember to give trading your 100% focus, losing your costly bitcoins by making mistakes when trading is not ideal. Focus and check your facts and you will make the most of your trading experience.

Chapter 5: How Bitcoin Mining Works

Bitcoin mining for profit and investment is an extremely competitive field and in order to do so you have to follow some steps to ensure you can mine safely and profitably.

If you are a professional coder and have experience Linux or Ubuntu, then you may feel that your mining experience may be enhanced by using an established platform such as Genesis. Genesis mining is one of the leading cloud mining companies and provides the best option for smart ways to invest.

Join the team of experts and take advantage of the bitcoin mining algorithm that has been designed to provide rentals that can be used to mine in an efficient and reliable way.

Chances are you are more interested in a way for the individual with limited experience to enter the field of bitcoin mining.

It has to be pointed out that in the past mining could be done with an ordinary computer, but as the niche has become so competitive you will need to use ASIC miners, that's application specific integrated circuit to you and me, in order to mine successfully. Details of how you can obtain this hardware are available on the internet and you should be able to pick up what you need.

Firstly, we must ascertain if the process of bitcoin mining is even capable of producing a profit when applied to your circumstances. This can be worked out with a bitcoin mining calculator.

Once you have your mining calculator on your screen you will need to enter your mining hardware hash rate in GH/s, your power wattage and the cost of your electricity in dollars per Kw per hour. The calculator will automatically insert the level of difficulty, block reward and current bitcoin price.

Once the data has been entered you will receive a number of sets of figures. The calculations will be as follows

1. How many days it will take to generate one block of BTC with solo mining

2. How many days to generate a single bitcoin

3. How many days will it take to not see a loss

It is worth noting that all of these figures can vary greatly depending on exchange rates and sometimes just old-fashioned luck! These figures should also be taken as a guideline and should not be used to invest money. Any money used to invest in mining must be classed as "spare cash" due to the uncertainty and various variables that applies to the process.

You have now done your calculations and have decided you want to take this route. Time to choose your miner. There is plenty of material in the form of hardware reviews that can be used to help you make an informed choice.

Before we go any further a bitcoin wallet is needed, a fairly straightforward process. If you visit Bitcoin's site there are a host of alternative to choose from. In order to use your wallet for mining you will need to know your public address and not your private key.

Now we need to find a mining pool. It is not advised to mine individually as it is very unlikely that you will come across a bitcoin block and since that is how the currency is awarded, usually in a block of 12.5 at a time you will have more success when working as a group.

Choosing your pool is a very important part of the process. Below are the considerations that you must consider when choosing your pool.

1. Pool fee: Many consider this to be the main consideration when choosing your pool. Normally the fees range from 0% to 4% and the standard fee is generally 1%. If you find a pool that has the same features as another but a lower fee then choose that one but keep an eye on the fee structure.

   a. It is also possible to find a pool that has a 0% fee, unusual but not unheard of. This would normally indicate a new pool that is looking to attract customers. Again, keep an eye on fee structures.

2. Payment system: General rule of thumb is determined by risk. If the pool operator is assuming the risk then it follows that they will pay a lower rate than a pool in which the miners assume the risk. This can also affect fee structure. Your first decision is to either accept a greater percentage of risk, pay less fees but accept that you may create less income. Alternatively, you could join a pool that guarantees a lower rate of profit but the pool operator guarantees payment for every proof of work.

3. Minimum payout: When choosing a pool, you will need to check out the payout period, the minimum payout and who is responsible for transaction fees. By determining if it is the pool or the user who pays fees you can make informed choices.

4. Currency: Choosing the mining currency you wish to mine is a consideration you will need to address. Currently there are a number of alternatives. If you want to mix it up a little the multi-pool option may appeal to you. These allow mining of several crypto currencies at any time and can convert your profits into BTC once you decide to withdraw funds.

5. Geography: Always check your pool has servers in your country, or at least your continent! If they do check the URL for the servers and choose the one that allows you to mine more efficiently.

You will now need to get a mining program for your computer. If you have chosen a pool that already uses software like BitMinter then you are good to go. If, however the pool you have joined does not have its own software then you will need to choose your own.

Compare different mining software by checking the internet, two of the most popular programs are BFG miner and 50Miner.

All ready to go mining? Then let's begin! Connect your miner to the power and then attach it to your computer with a USB lead. Once you have opened up your mining software you will need to join your pool and enter your user name and password.

Once this is done you will begin mining for bitcoins, or your other chosen cryptocurrencies.

The actual process of mining is essentially releasing blocks of BTC by solving complex mathematical problems and algorithms. While there are millions of these equations surrounding each block of BTC not all of the equations have to be solved to release the block. This is where "chance" comes into play. You could unlock a block of BTC on the first, the hundredth or the millionth time you solve a problem.

The key is to find the winning equation that releases the block. How fast the problems are solved is determined by the speed and power of the computer solving it.

As a user, you are simply telling your computer that you want to mine, that is what the mining software is for, and at any one time there are tens of thousands of computers working on each equation at the same time and looking to release the same block of BTC. Therefore, it is suggested that you join a mining pool as opposed to working alone.

There has been four generations of mining hardware and modern miners are most likely to have dedicated mining rigs that are solely for the purpose of mining bitcoin.

Will there be a future without bitcoin mining? Simple answer- yes there will. It is believed that the final bitcoin will be produced by 2140 and as the final blocks are released there will be no more to reveal. Until then the number of people trying to mine currency grows every day and the chances of making a profit by this method becomes more difficult but that is the chance you take.

Bitcoin mining is a gamble, you will need to weigh up the pros and cons, examine the startup costs and decide if this is the route you want to take. If it is then happy mining and may your hard work bring you profit!!

Not your thing? Maybe you will be content simply buying currency and waiting for the price to rise. Whatever you decide then make sure you check out all information thoroughly.

Maintaining The Ledger

From a fundamental level and basic perspective BTC is simply a ledger with numbers and balances with state of the art tamper resistant security features. Anytime your engaging in a transaction your wallet app sends information to the bitcoin network describing how the network will change, this includes the account owner's personal info, account number and amount of BTC that are being transferred.

BTC requires a unique signature from the account owner to validate the authenticity of the transaction, synonymous to that of a hand written signature on a bank cheque, but the difference is this signature is based on unique code (mathematical equation). Each BTC account holder has a specific key affiliated with their account that only the account holder would know, and this is used to create unique signatures by encrypting certain transactional messages.

The bitcoin network will authenticate the signature by trying to decrypt it, and upon successful decryption it will verify that this signature belongs to the true account holder. These mathematical based signatures (equations) are unique and therefore cannot be duplicated to engage in other transactions.

So who is validating and continuously checking the accuracy of the ledger? The answer is anyone! I'll elaborate remember BTC is a decentralized system meaning nobody has ownership over it. It is an autonomous type of currency. Anytime a transaction occurs using BTC, the bitcoin network made up of ordinary people with computers which check the ledger automatically. Everyone apart of the bitcoin network has a copy of the ledger, and the reality is this bitcoin network is spread across the world. Thus, connection delays and occasionally "attempted fraud" does occur, how do we know what version of the ledger to use?

The bitcoin network uses a democratic type of system sort of like a ballot system, but with some differences. The computers on the bitcoin network also known as "nodes" solve complex mathematical equations based on their version of the ledger. Once a problem is solved the computer from the bitcoin network announces a solution and everyone updates to that version of that ledger. Note this is designed to favor the majority version, thus in this case the most accurate answer is the most consistent one among the bitcoin network.

Each puzzle is built on previous answers and this eliminates anyone trying to presolve a problem . Ergo, this operates on the principle of not the most recent solution, but the ledger version with the most consistent and total solutions.

How is money created? Anytime a math equation (verifying transactions) is solved a small reward is added to the balance of the computer that solved it. This functions as an incentive for people who help maintain the ledger through the bitcoin network. This was dubbed **"mining"** as computers would get rewarded for solving advanced mathematical equations. The fact is "miners" are in actual fact maintainers who's true purpose is to maintain the ledger!

This was all a clever and elaborate design to somehow distribute money all across the globe. Remember BTC are capped and are destined to reach the maximum threshold in the year 2140.

Summary

Advantages:

Decentralized system - Nobody has ownership, no authoritative institutions have control, and governments cannot intervene.

Utilizes BlockChain technology - Because BTC uses blockchain technology it makes this cryptocurrency tamper resistant and extremely difficult for fraud and any other shady transactions unlikely.

Hyper Ledger - utilizes a ledger that records every single transaction that occurs. Which can be used to trace transaction with pinpoint accuracy from point of origin to finish.

Finite Currency - BTC is a finite currency and has a cap. Meaning unlike banks, you cannot print out new money on demand. (this is what causes inflation - money loses value)

Accounts Cannot Be Frozen - It's a known fact that banks for whatever reasons, when they become suspicious of certain financial activity they have the right to either freeze your account or terminate it without any warning or legitimate reason. Don't believe me? Read the fine print the next time you sign up with whomever you decide bank with.

This has actually happened to a friend of mine before, he use to operate an event management company which was quite lucrative, and one time he was expecting a deposit of **250,000 USD** and even advised the branch manager at the time, but can you guess what happened? For whatever reason they still decided to flag his personal bank account and it was frozen for "further investigation" and there was absolutely nothing he could do about it.

He ran a legitimate business, and fortunately he did eventually get access to his bank account 2 weeks later, however imagine the amount stress and headaches he had to go through. He had to pay vendors, employees, and other expenses, yet he could not touch any of his money that he rightfully owned.

But with BTC accounts cannot be frozen. So if the same scenario went down with depositing BTC he would of had no hassle or any problems whatsoever.

No Prerequisites - Laws and regulations vary from country to country, however the fact is that banks have limits and arbitrary rules to control your money. With BTC all you need is an account, BTC wallet and an internet connection. That's all!

Direct Person To Person Transfer- With BTC there are no intermediaries, clearing houses or middlemen you find with traditional banks. I personally like this approach a lot better as large volume transactions can be done with ease, fluidly and efficiently with no long waiting times. Money can be received instantly.

Transaction Fees Significantly Decreased - Let's face it banks are not looking for the best interest of the people. Expensive transaction and hidden fees is something we are all constantly bombarded with, and can be costly. But with BTC you will face significantly reduced fees compared to banks.

Disadvantages

No customer technical or customer support - Since BTC runs on a decentralized system, when you run into trouble perhaps your hard drives crashes, you lost your password or unique key code, the fact is you have nobody to turn to. Banks would have customer support.

Bitcoin Value Volatile - Simply put the value of BTC can be erratic, and if someone hypothetically came up with a better cryptocurrency with a greater algorithm what happens to BTC? The value would surely drop, and thus BTC can be considered unstable for this reason.

Negative perceptions - Ever since the rise of "silk road" a black market website selling illegal goods in exchange for BTC, bitcoins got quite a bad rep due to the fact it was used as a veil for criminals to conduct commerce under.

Banks Do Not Support Bitcoin - The fact is BTC threatens the very existence of financial institutions and they do not at all like the fact that BTC a decentralized system and currency exists. Banks have terminated many accounts of users who engaged in mixing BTC with their bank accounts.

No Physical Properties - BTC in reality has no actual value, but just like any fiat currency it is given value by us. Remember BTC is intangible, it's not like gold, silver or copper.

Trigger Deflation - BTC could trigger deflation, meaning lower prices on goods and even wages. This could lead to people "hoarding money", less spending.

BTC is an electronic currency that is based on a unified maintained ledger. People transfer "bitcoin currency" by sending messages to the bitcoin network known as maintainers or "miners" who verify signatures in the form of complex math equations. Maintainers/miner do a general consensus to find out the accurate solution and verify the authenticity of the message from the account holder.

BTC in actual fact has no value, but achieves its value because we give it value just like any other fiat currency. BTC is a completely intangible substance unlike the physical currency we use today.

We must highlight an important aspect of BTC, and that's what happens if user error mistakes are made, such as hard drive crashes which stores your pertinent "key code information"? This will result in a permanent loss of BTC associated with the account holder's private key code.

Since its a decentralized system there is no technical support or bank teller assistance you can turn to, thus your BTCs are lost forever.

Chapter 6: Why does the Emergence of the CryptoCurrency Anger the Government?

As ordinary citizens we must recognize BTC's economic magnitude and political influence of the vested interests it directly threatens. It's quite clear BTCs will have opposition and perhaps create conflict of immense proportions within society. These "conflicts" will most likely straddle between decentralized cryptocurrency systems and mechanisms, and current centralized banking institutions who have their own agenda.

The perceptions on BTCs may vary from person to person, but entrenched interests of government bodies and financial banking institutions have a tunnel vision notion and that is BTCs could threaten the economy by making banking institutions obsolete, and in other words ushering in a new era of digital currency, that has no ownership nor belongs to any one third party. In essence the rise of BTC could bring forth the extinction of current banking and financial operating standards we live with today. But, is this necessarily a bad thing?

One of the main and considerably the biggest sticking points financial institutions use is that BTCs can trigger "deflation". However, again we must question is this necessarily a bad thing? Deflation fundamentally is a problem for government bodies, and not citizens. I'll elaborate, deflation implies a decrease in value and in this case it will have a ripple effect; pricing on goods would lower, and then due to equilibrium lower wages, and then last but not least this would put pressure on taxes, meaning lower taxes for people to pay! - This means less tax revenue for the government.

What do you think any government entity on this planet would say to "less tax revenue"? Last I checked lowering taxes is not a priority on any sane government's agenda. Have you ever faced a government union and requested to lower their wages? I don't think so, and it's quite clear this wouldn't be a viable option to any government party in existence.

Central banks and governments warn of the potential of being defrauded through cryptocurrencies. However, one could argue we are already being defrauded through current centralized banks via "inflation", this is when money is endlessly printed and decreases in value (buying power).

If BTCs becomes widespread worldwide banking institutions could not use interest rates and quantitative easing to manipulate the economy as they see fit, meaning they cannot manage the economy. Last I checked I don't ever recall a time in history where the economy as a whole was completely stable? On the contrary there have always been high peaks and deep dips, think about it for a second.

Did You know: Both complexes of financial institutions and governments rely on banking fees which I am sure you are more than familiar with, to generate revenue in the billions! Below you can see an example of some current fees central banks charge people.

Centralized Banking Fees

- Deposit

- Withdrawal

- Escrow

- Trust management

- Foreign exchange

- Collection

Simply put, whoever controls currency controls power. Over the last few decades the government has become a larger part of all our lives. Irrelevant of the party in power there is the feeling that we are all living in a "nanny state" and many people are rebelling against this concept.

The reality is that the government is acting like an all seeing "Big Brother" type presence. The overwhelming need to watch and track us, controlling all our movements and data the government is increasingly intrusive and invasive. Unfortunately, we are brought up with a belief that the government has our best interest at heart. From cradle to grave we rely on the people in power to address problems in society and mend them.

Too many of us accept that the government is the ultimate authority and fail to question the extent of their influence over all we do. We will address the ways that our government control our money and businesses and just how the introduction of the crypto currency can go a long way to taking back our basic rights!

To various levels of government, the ordinary man in the street is basically a source of revenue. It would seem that our primary function is to provide money via taxes. Be it federal, state or local we are bombarded with taxes. Also, the government has the right to regulate money as well as having the power to regulate the value of local and foreign money.

Businesses are now swamped with red tape; the Federal Register is a classic indication as to the use of regulations and how it has grown over the years. The Register had 2,500 pages in 1936 but today boasts an impressive 80, 000 plus pages!

It is no wonder that many people will not even attempt to enter any entrepreneurial arena. The government has couched all activities connected with small business in red tape and mind-boggling regulations and convoluted policies.

It can be said that the exploding welfare state is taking away our independence. Too often individuals are brought up to believe that they are fundamentally unable to care for themselves. Once living in poverty becomes the norm it is very hard to climb out of the hole you find yourself in. The government provides a level of care with welfare and a rapidly growing number of people accept that they are dependent on the state to survive.

Your independence is often provided with a number of basic needs. So how can BTC and the dawn of digital currency alter this?? Put simply it can aid even the poorest person to have a basic means of buying goods they wish to purchase.

Today's society requires a level of credit in order to take part in normal day to day activities. Often booking a hotel room or shopping online are impossible to do without a credit card, simple transactions that most of us take for granted, but the reality is this is extremely difficult for people who are living on the threshold of poverty.

Having a bank account requires permission from officials, someone somewhere must judge you and your "right" to have this seemingly basic requirement. Cryptocurrency requires absolutely no permission from anyone. If you have money and the means to download you can set up an online wallet and enter the world of commerce and trade.

As the number of outlets that are accepting various forms of cryptocurrency increase the banks are losing their grip on trading. It will take a while, but forward thinking people are already talking about a time when this new digital age is the way the majority of trades will take place.

Bitcoin and its use in other countries also makes the cost of travelling more affordable and open to the lower earning classes. By removing exchange rates between countries and introducing a global rate of currency BTC is opening doors and markets to people who have been excluded previously.

Relinquishing any form of control is unpalatable to today's government. The age of control has for many years been increasing, consider the various ways the state monitors our lives.

1. The FDA has complete control over all food supplies. With the introduction of broadly written acts that are vaguely worded it is possible that in the future all our food supplies and safety issues will be controlled completely by the government.

2. Health care. Due to major changes in health care laws there are incredibly constraining regulations regarding the types of health insurance available in place for people who meet a specific criteria. Once more the government dictates our lives!

Blockchain and its properties can regulate and clean up the voting process. In this age of accusations of vote rigging, underhand behavior and generally undemocratic practices it has long been believed that there is no way to conduct a secure and honest vote online. Blockchain has altered this thinking and may well be a way to make sure all future elections are transparent and free from corruption.

The crisis that occurred in Cyprus in 2012-2013 when banks figuratively took their gloves off and joined with the government to prevent moving of capital ($) by islanders, opened up a lot of people's eyes. While it was generally believed that capital control was a thing of the past, by joining forces the banks and the government put its collective foot down and maintain their far reaching authority.

This was an enlightening event and the world watched on in wonder, mostly believing it could never happen to them. It began to dawn on society that, guess what?? It can happen anywhere! Part of the appeal of the digital currency is that it takes the power over our money away from the government and that gives them just one more reason to dislike the properties of BTC. Any loosening of the ties that bind us to banks and central government can only be good for our personal choices and society as a whole.

In essence people will gain a new type of autonomy that extends beyond the confining reach of government, banks and centralized power. Remember bitcoin is decentralized currency and works in a system that is transparent, reliable and accurate. Governments have been established for one purpose and that's to control, regulate and dictate society on a whim.

The very existence of government bodies and even centralized banking authorities is actually in fact threatened in this digital era we find ourselves in. Look at the freedom we have with the internet in terms of communication, purchasing power, etc. BTC will be a new wave of change that will effect and shift the tides of power and tip it into the hands of people and create a leveled playing field for the common person.

Can you see why governments and other authoritative figures dislike the idea of a decentralized system and Bitcoin currency? BTC shifts the power into the hands of the people, and has various failsafe measures that make it feasible for real world application. Think about it, banks can print as much money as they please at any given time, and sure they will be cautious to do so due to inflation, but this is besides the point. The fact is they have the option to print money on demand on a whim or if they see fit, and this sort of power is solely theirs!

With BTC there is a limit with how much is in existence and this caps the amount of currency available. BTC are capped at 21 million and it is estimated to reach its limit in the year 2140. This means you cannot artificially create or manipulate currency once it has been set, unlike centralized banks who can print money on demand. Remember ownership belongs to no one, and thus this is an independent and autonomous currency.

Throughout history we can see the control of any given society or populace through the means of religion, money and goods. In this case bitcoin attempts to stem the tide of centralized control, regulation and perhaps even social stratification. This cryptocurrency will allow people from all walks of life, even from the poorest of families to contribute to society productively. Remember some isolated villages untouched by the western influence do not have access to banks, proper documentation and other regulatory frameworks that align us with government.

By now I bet your wondering what the future holds for BTC? Can government bodies and financial institution really stop this enigmatic, autonomous and reliable cryptocurrency? If I had to play devil's advocate, and be on the other side of the spectrum, there are a few things I would do to halt the existence of BTC.

The most strategic way governments can interfere with BTC business is by getting a foothold through "regulation", and we all know what this means. Any time governments regulate something they set frameworks, policies and complex procedures to keep the common person out by setting boundaries and a criteria. There have already been attempts of licensing procedures for BTC, but I cannot say for sure if governments will be successful doing so. Time will tell, and in the mean time stock up on BTC and continue to ride the wave of freedom!

BONUS - BITCOIN HISTORY

Although the history of BTC is somewhat obscure the estranged man behind both the development of BTC and the initial stages of blockchain is Satoshi Nakamoto. This all started approximately in the year 2008. It is believed Mr. Nakamoto posses *1 million* BTC that have a cash value of **2.7 billion USD**!! (Present year 2017)

The group of people who assisted in the development of BTCs is still an enigma and there is a lot of mystery that shrouds this question even today, however we do know for certain that Mr. Nakamoto and his group of developers intended to have some sort of new electronic cash system implemented during economic crisis between the years 2007 - 2008. This was an extremely strategic and clever ploy trying to leverage the world's economic turmoil and capitalize on it by introducing a totally radical, new, unparalleled, and revolutionary currency.

This cryptocurrency would be the first ever intangible form of money that only exists in "cyberspace". BTC has its limits, and by that I mean it is a finite currency and capped at a maximum threshold of 21 million to be brought into existence. Meaning once that cap is reached no more BTC can ever be produced.

There is a lot of controversy surrounding the true identity of Mr. Satoshi Nakamoto or if this is even a real person. There are a lot of speculations ranging from being someone from "common wealth origins" to being a Japanese - American born systems engineer, I cannot give a definitive answer to this conjecture. But, what I can say is ever since the debut of BTC it has been continuously gaining upward momentum and shows no signs of slowing down and is currently worth *2739.26 USD* per BTC! That's right, $2739 USD for a single bitcoin! (current value estimated **July 2017**)

Obviously just like any market share value will fluctuate due to various factors in the free market. Therefore, you can expect big spikes and deep declines, but I can say BTC is most definitely a lucrative prospect and something worthwhile investing in. It is a currency that is here to stay for the foreseeable future and will continue to impact the lives of millions of people worldwide.

BTC has made more than a handful of people millionaires, including myself. How was this done? Simply put I zoned in on an opportunity, saw a trend and predicted the future based on past patterns. Not difficult at all right? Perhaps I used a bit of "chance" too, I was in the right place at the right time. In all honesty, when it comes to capitalizing on trends you must be able to discern, time, and take massive action towards it, and then you will be rewarded with fruition from the risk you took. Before BTC gained its high value, when youtube videos, blogs on BTC, and "How to do" books /articles weren't around, BTC's value was worth less than a fraction of its value today.

Me and many others purchased BTC when they were priced around $14 -$35 USD per BTC. As you can see the price has exponentially increased and those who invested early as always reap massive results! Now you're probably questioning is it too late to join in on the "BTC gold rush"? My answer is, NO. There is still a massive opportunity that exists to make a killing and capitalize on this BTC trend.

I get this type of question all the time and I always answer by responding with a few questions of my own, would you tell someone who's never used the internet or smart phone it's too late? It's too late to start your own online venture (business) on the net or learn how to become more tech savvy? It's too late to upgrade from you "old school" flip phone to a smart phone? Can you see my logic? Of course it's not too late! And there are multi millionaires still being made currently as I speak, and there are more to come in the foreseeable future, 2-5 years and beyond.

The more saturated the market is the more competitive it gets, and the more challenging it gets for you to make immense profits, however that does not eliminate the potential possibilities to make high yielding returns on your investment. At the moment I would say there is so much room for growth and the market is nowhere near saturated yet. Therefore, after you finish reading this book I strongly suggest you take my advice and put it into practice. Taking massive action is key to obtaining long term and consistent success. You do not want to take high stake gambles obviously, but, make an informed decision and take "measured risks".

Historical Trends

Since the history of mankind technological advancements that spurred waves of monumental change shaped the world in which we live today, such as the renaissance, industrial age, etc. At any given period of time in history we see patterns, trends and paradigms that shape the world we live in today.

BTC will be the next BIG trend and will shift government policies, regulations, and legislation forever. Imagine a decentralized system with no authoritative institutions s in control, no detrimental government intervention, but only the will of the people manifested through an autonomous currency. Isn't this incredible?

Of course people will be skeptical at first, but as we look at history's historical trend we can see anytime massive change or revolution occurs it was always met with opposition, consisting of people who are skeptic about change. Anytime new knowledge or technology was implemented it was always mocked, ridiculed and even denied.

Please see below an excerpt from the book Blockchain Technology & Blueprint Ultimate Guide. You can see recent historical events that occurred that continue to change the world for the better in which we live today..

"We live in the digital age and it would only make sense that currency would eventually follow in the transition into the digital realm, ie: cryptocurrency. This is not merely speculation or abstract conjecture, but this is based on trends and a few facts. Let's take a look at some of the things we interface with on a daily basis that have also stepped into the world digitization."

Books - In the past libraries were the only source to get access to books and other information packages. But, now we have digital books (kindle, Kobo,etc).

Music/Podcasts - Before you had to buy records, tapes, and CDs to listen to your favorite artist. Now we have itunes and other platforms that allow you to instantly listen to music without having to go through the hassle of buying an actual physical product. Digital access to music eliminates the damaged merchandise factor, for example a scratch on a CD would render the music on it inaudible, meaning you would have to go buy another copy! With music being digital you eliminate such inconveniences.

Video Games - Synonymous to music this too has stepped into the digital era. Games use to be purchased on cartridges and most recently CDs, but now can all be downloaded at the touch of a button online for instant access.

Mail - Before the invention of the E-mail the vast majority of people in society solely relied on mail couriers (mail men/women) as a means of relaying communication. However, since the advent and successful launch of the E-mail people now communicate worldwide with lightning speed! Uninterrupted by time zones and other external factors.

Bill Payments - In the past the average person had to rely on cheques to get paid and to exchange large volumes of cash in any given transaction. Bills would have to be paid by cheque, and the period of waiting times were immensely long. But, now we have direct deposits (Electronic Wire Transfers) and other similar electronic deposits. We can even make bill payments and purchases directly from our smart phones!

As you can see the above historical trends, some more recent than others indicates quite a few things, 1. accessibility and autonomy is an increasing trend, and 2. Evolution is an inevitable variable and we must adapt accordingly. It's only a matter of time when currency also follows in the digital paradigm. After all this is the digital age, right?

Silk Road

Whether your liberal, conservative or in between everyone holds an opinion on BTC and other cryptocurrencies. Views range on the scale from either positive, in-between or negative, and depending on your socio-economic status and beliefs your most likely one of the three options.

BTC has received some negative limelight in the past and was considered money for "criminals" and a safe haven for them as the anonymity aspect behind BTC concealed their personal details. "Silk Road" was a black-market website that criminals used to exploit BTC to exchange currency for illegal goods, such as firearms, drugs, and other contraband. Since BTC operates on a decentralized system this make it hard for authorities to track down criminals whom purchased illegal goods. Whereas centralized systems like our current banks would leave a paper trail behind each transaction for authorities to follow.

The website was eventually shut down by the FBI, and a tainted name for BTC stigmatized a number of people in the process. The negative perception still remains, however I cannot concur with the blind negative sweeping statements made about cryptocurrency. Sure certain attributes of BTC attract criminal elements to the fore, but this does not make BTC intrinsically "evil" or bad. I'll elaborate, our current currency the "almighty dollar"(USD) is known to be used for the same exact illegal purchases made with BTC, such as guns, narcotics, human trafficking, etc. So how can you rightfully single out BTC when the USD is used in the same fashion? This is both contradictory and hypocritical if you think about it.

What justification is there to negatively distinguish one currency form from another, when both currencies are still utilized by criminals? How does this make one currency better than the other? The only differences I see is one currency is decentralized and another is centralized.

Psychology of Money

In this bonus sub chapter I'd like to discuss the psychology of money and the rigid conceptions people have on this subject matter. I've briefly mentioned in previous chapters how money obtains its value, and the fact is we give all currencies value whether digitally decentralized or fiat.

In the past we depended on agriculture to survive, but as time progressed and through advanced agriculture technology only a small sect of people engage in this "lost art". Most of us here in industrial societies go to our local supermarket to buy goods in exchange for our money. We have internalized the concept that this centralized medium found in the forms of paper, coins and cheques is what keeps society afloat. I'm sure we've all heard of the term "money makes the world go round", right?

After all money is the driving force that keeps people working their 9-5, responsible for political processes, lobbying, and let's not forget war. It's the very infrastructure that maintains our fully functional society, so it makes sense when a new currency is introduced, BTC to be precise. It is met with vehement opposition because it threatens old customs and antiquated notions.

Money can be thought of as a matrix or nucleus that connects to every facet of our lives within society, subtly interwoven in almost every aspect of life you can think of. BTC removes central banks from sticking their noses where it doesn't belong and prevents government intervention which has brought great economic turmoil in the past. (bail outs)

Although BTC is inherently an intangible form of currency, we must shift our thinking to understand that money does not necessarily need to have a physical form in order to be utilized or retain value. We attribute value to our current monetary system, for example the $100 bill only has value because we associate it proportionally to its market value in whatever state you reside.

The use of credit/debit cards to purchase goods is evidence enough to validate an electronic monetary system that works and is reliable. So if credit/debit cards work on similar electronic principles, why can't implementing BTCs work as well? With BTCs you would have the simplicity of easy direct person to person money transfer, and the security edge of blockchain technology which would record and authenticate all transactions that take place.

We as a human species need to collectively expand our horizons and open our minds to new innovations and opportunities that will be the catalyst to massive change for the betterment of humanity as a whole. The archaic perception of what money is needs to be left behind in the past, and we need to embrace the digital age of intangible BTC.

Conclusion

Whatever your approach to the new digital era you will now be able to make informed choices. It is clear that the cryptocurrency world is developing at fast rate and our level of involvement will vary from person to person.

Maybe the thrill of the exchanges appeal to you, possibly you have tried traditional methods of stock trading and want to check out the hype surrounding the fluctuating new asset that is BTC, if that is so then enjoy the ride!

If you are lucky enough to own a computer that has the necessary specs to allow you to join a team of bitcoin miners then maybe you will get lucky and be in a team that answers that one problem that unlocks the block.

If neither of the above appeals to you there is the more traditional ways to purchase currency and wait for it to increase in value. Use the methods we have covered to watch trends and perhaps predict highs and lows in prices. This can be incredibly rewarding and by using charts to map prices and trends you can develop a knack for spotting upward movement of price.

Using the media coverage of BTC you can see for yourself how different stories impact on price. Join one of the many forums that are out there discussing the whole bitcoin phenomenon. Social media has embraced the idea of crypto currency and the future it can hold, try using your different platforms such as Twitter and Facebook and you may be surprised at the interest you can raise and the varied sources it will come from.

The message to take with you is to enjoy your interaction with the new digital world of currency, and believe me this new trend is here to stay, as they say knowledge is power!!

See below other recommended books written by Raymond Kazuya:

Blockchain Technology & Blueprint Ultimate Guide

LINK: http://amzn.to/2sQKeyM

Investing in Etherum Cryptocurrencies & Profiting Guide

LINK: http://amzn.to/2uuGVt9

GLOSSARY (words to know)

Cryptocurrency - is any type of digital currency that uses complex encryption technology and algorithms.

Bitcoin (BTC) - digital currency used like any other fiat currency to exchange, purchase and engage in commerce.

Hyper Ledger - An open data base that records all transactions.

Quantitative Easing - when central banks purchase any form of securities whether from government or the market in order to maintain lower interest rates and increasing the supply of money.

Inflation - when any currency loses its value or "buying power", and the general increase in price of products, goods and services.

Blockchain - in essence is a digital ledger used in BTC and other cryptocurrencies that creates a permanent and irreversible record for public access.

"Silk Road" - black-market website that sold contraband in exchange for BTC, which was eventually shut down by the FBI.

GLOSSARY (continued..)

Centralized Banking - current institutions we live with today, whom have control and ownership over the dollar.

Decentralized currency - BTC is a prime example of a decentralized currency which is autonomous and belongs to no one.

Volatile - unstable and fluctuates up and down.

Trends - patterns that indicate some sort of increase or decrease, and gives a general idea of the direction or development, and change of something.

Fiat Currency - legal tender that has its value backed by government, and much like any currency it is given its value by the market. A good example would be the USD or EU.

Mining - Miners in actual fact are "maintainers" of the ledger system BTCs utilizes. This term "miner" was coined due to the nature of the tasks, computers on the BTC network would solve complex math equations resulting in verifying the authenticity of a transaction, and as an incentive the computer that solved the equation first was rewarded with a portion of BTC.

Deflation - A reduction within the economy that effects wages, taxes, pricing, etc. Can be considered a ripple effect that touches every aspect of the economy.

Interest Rates - an amount of interest due for a specific period of time and this is directly proportioned to what is borrowed or deposited.

Threshold - the maximum point or extent for a proceeding reaction, phenomenon or results that follows.

Algorithm - set of rules that are used to perform complex calculations, usually conducted by a computer.

BLOCKCHAIN TECHNOLOGY

& BLUEPRINT ULTIMATE GUIDE

LEARN EVERYTHING YOU NEED TO KNOW FOR BEGINNERS & EXPERIENCED

RAYMOND KAZUYA

Blockchain Technology & Blueprint Ultimate Guide:

Learn Everything You Need to Know
For Beginners & Experienced

Contents

Introduction

Most of us have heard of Bitcoin but how many of us are aware of the technology that underlies it – the blockchain. The blockchain is one of the most forward-thinking crypto technologies of today's digital world. While it started life as the backbone for Bitcoin, the blockchain has gone on to become the technology of choice for any decentralized, distributed consensus system.

The blockchain itself is nothing more than a public ledger, a ledger of transactions that is so transparent, everyone can see what is going on, every step of the way. We all know about authentication, especially on the internet. We all have to use passwords to sign in, we all have to prove who we are when we do something or pay for something and each of these activities is regulated by a central system. Think of your bank account; your salary goes in, your bills are paid by a debit system and your account is maintained, accessible online or in a bank. All of this is regulated by a financial services authority, in this case, your bank, and everything you do is monitored and tracked electronically. Everything is kept confidential and secure but someone else still has control of your money.

With the blockchain, while every transaction is secure and confidential, the only person that has any control is you and you alone. The blockchain also solves another problem – with centralized systems, it costs money and the transactions take time. With the blockchain, each transaction costs a tiny fraction of what a centralized system would charge and each transaction is instant. You can send money from one side of the world to the other in a split second and, while you can already do this with services like PayPal, the costs of the blockchain are much lower.

Throughout this book, you will become familiar with blockchain. We will be looking at the concepts that keep it secure, such as public and private keys, digital signatures and hashing. We will be looking at how the blockchain is kept secure, the technology that underlies it, making it one of the most trusted systems in the world, safe from malicious users and with no chance of being hacked.

We are going to look at what the blockchain could be used for in the future and what it is used for now; we take a look at the most famous use case of the blockchain – Bitcoin, and what makes it tick, how it all works. And we are going to take a look at how blockchain is going to change the world, the financial world, as we know it.

The blockchain is not a simple ledger although what you see when you look at it may look simple. It is complex, full of algorithms, checking mechanisms to ensure security and it goes much deeper and much further than any other financial system. By the end of this book, you will be well-versed in what blockchain is and what it does, how it operates and, perhaps more importantly, why it works so well, why so many governments and financial institutions are likely to take up the use of the blockchain in the near future. Even more importantly, you will have an understanding of how blockchain can benefit you and your future!

Chapter 1: Cryptography

What is cryptography? It is an ancient art, one of codes, of secret writing, we've all seen the spy movies, some of us will even have written is secret code when we were younger. But the very first use of cryptography can be documented back to around 1900 BC, when non-standard hieroglyphs were used in an inscription by a scribe. There are those who argue the art of cryptography was a spontaneous result of the invention of writing, with uses from diplomatic messages to battle plans. It shouldn't come as any surprise to know that a new form of cryptography appeared after computer communication became more widespread. Let's face it, we should all know that, if we are communicating across a medium that is not trusted, we need some form of cryptography to keep what we are doing private and secure.

Today, cryptography is used for five main functions:

1. **Privacy and Confidentiality -** To ensure that only the intended recipient can read a message.

2. **Authentication** – to prove your identity

3. **Integrity** – to reassure the recipient that the message is exactly as you sent it and has not been changed.

4. **Non-repudiation** – a mechanism put in place to prove that you sent the message and it hasn't been intercepted.

5. **Key Exchange** – the way in which cryptography keys are shared between the sender and the recipient.

Cryptography always begins with plaintext data, data that is unencrypted. This is encrypted and becomes ciphertext and this will be unencrypted back to plain text. This encryption/decryption is always based on a key and on the cryptography scheme in use.

$C = E_k(P)$
$P = D_k(C)$

In this formula:

- P is plaintext

- C is ciphertext

- E is the encryption method used

- D is the decryption method used

- K is the key

Three terms that you will come across and that you must NOT confuse are:

- **Cryptography** – the encryption/decryption of messages through mathematical algorithms
- **Cryptanalysis** – the analyses and breaking of the encryption schemes
- **Cryptology** – Covering both above, this is the study of secret writing

3 Cryptographic Algorithms

There are several ways for cryptographic algorithms to be classified and these are the three most common ways, based on how many keys are used for the encryption/decryption and by their use and application:

- **SKC – Secret Key Cryptography** – a single key is used for encryption and decryption – often known as symmetric encryption and is used for confidentiality and privacy

- **PKC – Public Key Cryptography** – separate keys are used for encryption and decryption – often known as asymmetric encryption and is used mostly for key exchange, non-repudiation and authentication purposes

- **Hash Functions** – these encrypt information irreversibly using mathematical transformations, providing a kind of digital fingerprint. These are usually used for proving integrity of messages

Basic Principles of Cryptography

There are four basic principles of cryptography:

1. **Encryption**

Simply put, encryption is all about converting data into a form that is not readable by the human eye. This protects our privacy while the message is sent between two people. The recipient gets the decrypted version of the message that is encrypted when the sender sends it. Encryption and decryption require the use of a key, sometimes the same key, although usually different keys are required.

2. **Authentication**

Authentication is what makes sure the message comes from who it claims to come from. Let's say that Alice sends Bob a message; Bob wants to know that the message really came from Alice. Alice can perform an action on the message that Bob knows only she can do – that is the fundamental basis of authentication.

3. **Integrity**

One of the biggest issues faced by communication systems is a loss of integrity from messages that are being sent between people. Use of a cryptographic hash ensures that the messages are not intercepted and changed along the path of communication.

4. **Non-Repudiation**

What would happen if Bob received a message from Alice but she says she never sent it? Digital signatures are one way that cryptography is used to make sure this cannot happen

Different Cryptography Types

Earlier, I told you what the three main types of cryptography were and now I will go into a little more detail on each one.

1. **SKC – Secret Key Cryptography – Symmetric Encryption**

With the secret key method of encryption, just one key is used for the encryption and the decryption. A sender will encrypt a plaintext message using the key and turn it into ciphertext. This is then sent to the recipient and the same key will then decrypt the message back into plaintext so it can be read. The key must be known by both parties and is the secret to this form of encryption.

SKC schemes are usually known as stream or block ciphers. A stream cipher works on one byte at a time and puts a mechanism in place for feedback so the key changes constantly. Two of the more common stream ciphers are:

- **Self-Synchronizing** – These ciphers will calculate every bit in a key string. They are calculated as functions of the previous n-bit and are called as such because the decryption process stays synchronous with the encryption process by knowing how far it is into the n-bit keystream.

- **Synchronous** – these stream ciphers will generate a key stream that is independent of the message stream, but through the use of the same keystream generation with both the sender and the recipient.

Block ciphers encrypt data a block at a time and use the same key with each block. The difference between the two ciphers is that, with a block cipher, the plaintext message always encrypts to an identical ciphertext when the same key is used whereas, with the stream cipher, the plaintext encrypts to a different ciphertext each time.

2. **PKC – Public Key Cryptography – Asymmetric Cryptography**

It is claimed that PKC is the most significant of all cryptographic developments in the last 400 years. This kind of cryptography depends on one-way functions. These are mathematical functions that compute easily as opposed to the inverse function which is more difficult. Look at these examples:

- **Multiplication and Factorization** - Let's say you have a pair of prime numbers, 3 and 7, and you want to calculate the product of those numbers. This should be simple; the product is 21. Now let's suppose that you have a number which is the product of two prime numbers, 21 and you need to work out what the prime factors are. Eventually, you will work them out but it will take you a quite some time to factor than to multiply.

- **Exponentiation and Logarithms** – Let's say that you have the number 3 and you take it to the 6th power. Once again, this is relatively easy to work out – 3 to the power of 6 is 729. But what if you started with 729 and needed to work out what the x and y integers were so that log x 729 were equal to y. This will take much longer to calculate.

These may be reasonably trivial examples but they are representative of the functional pairs that PKC uses – the ease of exponentiation and multiplication and the more difficult tasks of calculating logarithms and factoring. The real "trick" to PKC is in finding the hidden door in a one-way function so that, when we know some information, the inverse calculation is easier.

PKC generally uses two related keys. However, although they are related, knowing what one key is doesn't automatically mean that you can work out what the other is. One encrypts the plaintext and the other key decrypts the ciphertext. What is important is that it makes no difference which order the keys are applied in, just that both are required. This is where the moniker 'asymmetric encryption' comes in.

One of the keys is a public key and whoever owns it can advertise it as much as they want. The other is a private key and is never told or revealed to anyone else. Sending messages using PKC is easy. Alice uses Bob's public key to encrypt a message and Bob will use his private key to decrypt it. Doing it this way, authentication and non-repudiation come into play.

3. **Hash Functions**

Hash functions are also known as one-way encryption or message digests. They are algorithms that do not use any key; instead, a hash value of fixed length is generated based on the plaintext. This means it is not possible for the length or the content of the plaintext message to be recovered. A hash function provides a digital fingerprint of the contents of a file and this is used to make sure that the file is not tampered with or altered in any way. These are used by operating systems for password encryption.

That is cryptography in a nutshell, the basics of encryption and encryption and the system used by the blockchain to ensure the integrity of every single transaction.

Chapter 2: Autonomy

The definition of autonomy is "freedom from external control or influence" and that defines the essence of blockchain. Nobody owns the blockchain; there is no central regulating or governing body, nobody to 'interfere' in the way it runs. The blockchain is completely independent, unlike the physical cash in your pocket which is owned by the bank, which is printed by the bank for as long as the government gives them permission to print it.

If that's the case, how does the blockchain work? How can it work so smoothly, be so secure when nobody governs it? The answer to that lies in the self-regulation mechanism within the blockchain and that mechanism is called distributed consensus.

What is Distributed Consensus?

It is a term that you will see often in conjunction with the blockchain and with cryptocurrency and it is claimed that solving distributed consensus is the innovation behind Bitcoin and enabled the explosion of alternative currencies or 'alt coins' as they are known. Consensus refers to a process of collective decision-making or where two or more people come to an agreement over what may be true or false. The term is used here in the same way as you would use it in your daily life. One group can come to a decision or a consensus without the need for every person in the group to be unanimously in support.

When a group of electronic devices or computers need to agree with one another about something so that they can operate, there is one central unit who will make the decision and then let the rest of the network know. However, what distributed consensus means is that the computers that make up the network, called nodes, all agree in a way that is more like a group of humans coming to an agreement and that means that each member of the group will come to one collective decision. Similar to how we have a jury in court that collaboratively work together on a verdict if a suspect is guilty or innocent.

What is difficult to grasp is how the network nodes from that distributed consensus operate, and that is even harder to do when one of the nodes is deliberately attempting to manipulate all the others or is lying.

Blockhain is here to stay and establishes a transparent system and methodology of engaging in business transactions that cannot be altered and can be easily accessed by the general public for authentication purposes. By implementing this sort of technology we eliminate the many pitfalls we are faced with today in regards to fraud, embezzlement and other financial infringements.

This innovative technology eliminates the need of centralized and authoritative systems to dictate and regulate society. The future is here and now we can rely on a decentralized system to level out the playing field in the world we live in today. Think about it?

Blockchain technology uses what is called a hyper ledger which essentially records all transactions that occurs and is stored on the blockchain system. Imagine your bank statements, but in a more expansive and larger scope, every single little detail from small purchases to large is recorded. Worldwide access to the public means there will no longer be a need for a central system to regulate financial transactions, ie: Financial institutions, banks, etc.

We live in the digital age and it would only make sense that currency would eventually follow in the transition into the digital realm, ie: cryptocurrency. This is not merely speculation or abstract conjecture, but this is based on trends and a few facts. Let's take a look at some of the things we interface with on a daily basis that have also stepped into the world digitization.

Books - In the past libraries were the only source to get access to books and other information packages. But, now we have digital books (kindle, Kobo,etc).

Music/Podcasts - Before you had to buy records, tapes, and CDs to listen to your favorite artist. Now we have itunes and other platforms that allow you to instantly listen to music without having to go through the hassle of buying an actual physical product. Digital access to music eliminates the damaged merchandise factor, for example a scratch on a CD would render the music on it inaudible, meaning you would have to go buy another copy! With music being digital you eliminate such inconveniences.

Video Games - Synonymous to music this too has stepped into the digital era. Games use to be purchased on cartridges and most recently CDs, but now can all be downloaded at the touch of a button online for instant access.

Mail - Before the invention of the E-mail the vast majority of people in society solely relied on mail couriers (mail men/women) as a means of relaying communication.

However, since the advent and successful launch of the E-mail people now communicate worldwide with lightning speed! Uninterrupted by time zones and other external factors.

Bill Payments - In the past the average person had to rely on cheques to get paid and to exchange large volumes of cash in any given transaction. Bills would have to be paid by cheque, and the period of waiting times were immensely long. But, now we have direct deposits (Electronic Wire Transfers) and other similar electronic deposits. We can even make bill payments and purchases directly from our smart phones!

Not only that but we can even deposit cheques via apps through our phones electronically! (most big banks have this feature) Physical stores are starting to dwindle in size and their profit margins are greatly diminishing due to "online customers" , simply because in this day in age people value convenience and instant gratification above all things. Buying online saves you the hassle of traveling to the store, attempting to find parking, and the heartache of finding out the product you were looking for is out of stock.

The list goes on and on, but I would imagine you get the point by now, and can see a trend of digitization rapidly growing and shows no signs of slowing down. So take these examples as evidence of a potential shift and boom in cryptocurrency! Blockchain is the technology behind bitcoin and various other cryptocurrencies and the trend to adopt blockchain is inevitable.

There are a plethora of multimillion dollar companies investing into blockchain technology for good reason, as it is now being seen as the new building block of the foreseeable future.

When it comes to money people have to place their trust into a third party to facilitate a transaction. Blockchain utilizes complex algorithms, math and cryptography and a transparent open centralized data base. Thus, creating a record that can be authenticated by the general public. The potential for blockchain is boundless, and almost anyone with an internet connection would be able to utilize this technology.

The far reaching prowess and implications are endless, perhaps in the near future it will be used to efficiently collect taxes, help immigrants send money back home who don't have access to financial institutions, and much, much more!

Blockchain will be met with some opposition from governments, financial and legal institutions due to the nature of its autonomy. With any new advancements we must embrace it and hold it to the utmost accountability, the revolution of blockchain technology is here and it is up to us to enable it.

At any period of time in civilization it's a known fact any new ideas, notions, knowledge and even technology has been blasted with extreme scrutiny, will blockchain undergo the same? It's hard to say and give a conclusive answer to this question, but what I can say is people and huge corporations are investing in blockchain by the droves as the potential is there.

We all want a system that is transparent, where records could be stored, facts authenticated, and ultimately security is guaranteed. Blockchain technology enables us to have all these incredible features, storing information on a network of computers and distributing information. Meaning no one person has ownership over the system!

The people who utilize blockchain submit bundles of information/records known as "blocks" in a chronological irreversible chain (hence the name blockchain). Now I'd like to briefly discuss some highlights of the hyper ledger used within blockchain technology, we will discuss this more in depth further in the book.

Distributed

Since this ledger is distributed it works as an open data base which shares all records stored in the blockchain. Accessible to anyone around the world who has access to an internet connection, and no one person is privy to this information. When an item is purchased through blockchain it goes through a series of authentication processes by involving everyone who must give consent to the occurring transaction, and they will all posses every record, history and piece of data on the purchased item.

Authenticated

No transaction can be altered or added to the blockchain without being recorded permanently and would need the consent of all parties involved to verify it. This eliminates the risk any fraudulent activities.

Secure

How trustworthy is blockchain? Certificates of authenticity, real time records, and product details are all available to secure and authenticate any existing transaction. At the end of a transaction there is a auditable and transparent record of information that validates authenticity. It doesn't matter whether its gold, diamonds, food, contracts deeds, etc. Blockchain technology will transform the world, it speeds up processes, increases cash flow, lowers transaction costs, and ultimately establishes trust among users.

Practical Example

Gold a commodity that has held immense value since the beginning of human civilization. In regards to commerce the framework of complex intermediaries involved surrounding gold can be quite overwhelming and time consuming, ranging from legal, regulatory, quality assurance, financial, and manufacturing bodies.

You have to run through a labyrinth consisting of government officials, lawyers, accountants, banks, sellers and middlemen. This is the current standard in which we operate in today and is an insecure methodology of practice to say the least. Smuggled gold or unethically derived gold can arise and be sold under the radar without any assurance.

However, blockchain technology will change all of that with what is known as a "hyper ledger". This will synchronize all transactions that occur and record each sequence from beginning to end. This technology enables us to trace the point of origin of gold from the mines right to the hands of consumers with pinpoint accuracy, transparency and reliability.

Blockchain technology, explained through

Bitcoin Distributed Consensus

The birth of Bitcoin came about from the thought that a network of digital currency could operate in a true P2P (peer to peer) manner, without any interference from any central authority. The potential here is that we can now reduce the reliance that we have on banks that claim to be too big to fail, banks who create and control new money for their own interests. That control would be placed squarely back in the hands of the people where it belongs.

In order for P2P money to work as it should, every network member needs to agree on the number of coins that all the other members own in order to prevent something called double-spending and to prevent fraud and theft.

Bitcoin, and by relation the blockchain, uses the process of "mining" to solve this distributed consensus problem. Any network member can decide to mine, but there is no requirement for you to become a miner in order to get some use out of the Bitcoin network. The miners are given rewards in the form of new Bitcoins and in 'older' Bitcoins that is paid by way of transaction fees from other network members.

The mining process uses 'Proof of Work' methodology to make sure that the consensus is correct and true. As well, it relies on game theory mechanics; this means that the design ensures that cheating and dishonesty is not in the best interests of any participant, even an incredibly selfish one. Let me try to put this in as simple a way as I can – each miner will perform an inordinate number of calculations. Each of these calculations will give the miner the opportunity to mine a transaction block, which contains all transactions that have taken place in a set time period and they can keep the reward that comes out of that block. However, for the network to accept the block, all the other miners on the network must confirm it or agree with the transaction history version on the network. The majority of that network will form the distributed consensus and this is done through the Proof of Work calculations and not the individuals.

If someone were to attempt to lie, the other miners would need to call them on it. Because each miner must maintain theory version of the history, it wouldn't be in their best interests to allow the lie to go through. This means that a malicious user could only manipulate the consensus to accept the fake transaction history by doing more proof of work calculations than all the rest of the network put together.

If a network member is not in agreement with the consensus, they will then 'fork' that network, creating another transaction branch history which will be different from the others. This will not be accepted by any user as a true part of the blockchain.

This means that the blockchain for Bitcoin depends on the hash-rate – this is how many calculations are performed by the network. They are called hashes simply because the mathematical name is 'secure hash algorithm'. If there are not many proof of work calculations being done, the entire network is considered insecure – any attacker would need to spend little to gain more than 50% of the hashing power and could then carry out a 51% attack. If large numbers are being performed, it could cost a lot more to buy the necessary computing power to do this. Because of the size of the network today, it would cost so much to carry out this attack that it simply wouldn't be practical nor profitable to do so.

Although I have talked mainly in terms of Bitcoin, simply because it was the first use, the above explains the self-regulating mechanism of any blockchain. It matters not what it is used for, only that it will work to secure the network no matter what.

Chapter 3: Practical Uses

The blockchain, as you now know, is the underlying technology for Bitcoin and other cryptocurrencies but, while these may be the headline-grabbers, the blockchain technology has moved further on and is now being adopted quite rapidly across a diverse selection of industries.

Because the blockchain is decentralized and because it is tamper-proof, it is the ideal technology for all different sectors and one area that it has been enjoying enormous success is in smart contracts. A smart contract is a piece of code that will run when conditions that are specifically defined are met. The uses of a smart contract are virtually limitless, especially where the result required is exchange. Many companies are now using these smart contracts in the supply chain to ensure the quality of their products and the dispatch of them.

What other industries could possibly adopt the blockchain technology though? Believe it or not, there are several practical uses for the blockchain and here are the five most exciting ones.

The Finance Sector

All the blockchain headlines have centered on cryptocurrency but in the meantime, the mainstream finance sector has been studying the blockchain technology for years and, now you know how it works, it's clear why they have been doing this. By using blockchain technology in their applications, they can significantly reduce the amount of time it takes for many internal processes and this will achieve three main things – a cut in costs and time, the elimination of third-party transaction recording and an increase in trust and security.

The Retail Sector

The retail sector is another that has long been researching this technology and its uses in the sector is increasing every day. By far the most valuable application for blockchain is in the guarantee of product, especially the high-value products like art and diamonds. Retailers are also in the forefront in their use of the blockchain to protect their customers from fraud. The potential for this technology is endless product tracking, item identification, location, time tracking, document management etc,. This functions similar to a QR code in regards to authentication and cannot be cheated.

The Agriculture Sector

Both farmers and the consumers are using blockchain technology to track a product from the first stage of rearing or growing right through to the end-purchase. It gives farmers the opportunity to ask for higher prices because they can guarantee their products are of quality and the consumers can see where their product has originated from with pinpoint accuracy.

The Insurance Sector

This is new era for blockchain technology, and is an exciting one too simply because the insurance industry spends, on average, around $2 billion every year on compliance and fraud prevention. Blockchain technology could make this process simpler by giving the insurance companies better access to data that is more reliable and by providing a link between the provider and the customer

The Energy Sector

Energy companies can use blockchain technology to provide consumers with complete transparency, allowing them to see exactly where their energy is supplied from, how it gets generated and how it is distributed. Consumers will also be able to make use of applications that are based on blockchain technology to gain accurate data about their use of energy, which will give them the ability to make more informed decisions and save money.

Business Case Studies

Blockchain technology safety lies in it being a distributed technology and not a centralized network. For the hacker, this means that getting access to sources of data means needing to hack into every single computer or node on the distributed network simultaneously – not the easiest of hacks! - Virtually impossible. The computing power that would be required for this kind of hack has previously been compared to being equivalent to the "hashing power of a nation state" along with all the tech companies in that nation state.

There are those that say the blockchain cannot be considered as a disruptive technology but is, instead, a foundational technology as it provides a structure and underlying framework for transactions in the future that involves anything of value. Let's have a look at some case studies and how blockchain technology could be put to use.

Case Study 1 – Banking

Our current banking systems are extremely vulnerable to fraud and recent example is Brazil. A group of hackers took over control of all the ATM and online operations of one of the largest Brazilian banks for several hours. In this time, they gained access to credit card information, passwords and a lot of other so-called secure information and anyone who logged in during that time was not aware they were being routed to a fake copy of the bank's site.

Middlemen like banks are not necessary with blockchain technology. The valuable information would not have been stored in a central access point, the bank website in this case, and it certainly wouldn't have been possible for the hackers to get access to all that information in those few hours.

Case Study 2 – Government Fraud and Corruption

US government officials were carrying out an investigation into extortion, theft and many other crimes on "Silk Road" on the internet. For those that don't know, the online Silk Road was an online darknet black market, originally used for drug selling and money laundering. The blockchain ledger that was in use turned up a very interesting fact – two of the FBI agents that were on the task force were, in fact, behind the criminal activity. The pair had tried to cover their tracks but, because blockchain is a publicly accessible ledger, that cannot be altered, and because it is decentralized, they couldn't hide from the truth or cover their tracks. The power of the blockchain lies in its ability to be completely transparent – nothing can be hidden from anyone.

The Pros and Cons of the Blockchain Technology

Everything has a good side and everything has a bad side and blockchain technology is no different. Here we look at the basic pros and cons of the technology:

Pros

- Anything that is of value may be transferred confidentially and safely, without risk of alteration
- All transactions are verified on a P2P network
- In times of economic crises, cryptocurrencies cannot be frozen like cash in your bank
- There will be no need for third-parties, like banks, government, lawyers, etc.
- No transaction can be reversed

Cons

- Scammers can use the anonymity of the technology for their own malicious use
- Manipulation and hacking is still possible, albeit on a small scale
- Most offices, governments, retailers, and others that deal with money have no real understanding of cryptocurrencies, let alone accept them as currency
- There is likely to be a great deal of resistance due to many people being employed in the middlemen jobs
- Transactions cannot be reversed

Going back to one of the downsides, because there are so many people employed by the banks, governments and other middlemen institutions, acceptance of blockchain technology won't be easy. However, these institutions are highly vulnerable to fraud, human error and corruption and this really does leave the door wide open for a better, safer way of carrying out transactions. At the end of the day, it is because there is so much fraud and corruption, not to mention the errors and the costs to the consumer that blockchain technology was created.

Be it banking, insurance, or any other industry, one thing is sure – we are going to see a lot of change in the future as these industries begin to adopt blockchain technology and, although it is expected to take many years for full adoption, businesses of today need to start planning now if they want to be on the cutting edge.

Risks of the Blockchain

Although blockchain technology offers a great deal of promise, adoption of it requires some very sound risk management to be put in place and that will require a full understanding of all the risks attached. Right now, the obvious risk revolves around Bitcoin and other cryptocurrencies on the blockchain, but as things evolve and new applications arise, those risks will change.

Take legacy insurance policies, for example. These might not have protection in place for a company that maintains bitcoin or any other blockchain asset and some may exclude anything to do with Bitcoin. Others might exclude digital currency or electronic data which means if your Bitcoin is lost, tough. You won't be able to claim on insurance for them!

There are other risks at consideration here – given that the value of Bitcoin fluctuates in fiat currency, how will their value be determined? And insurance isn't the only consideration; we also must consider regulatory risk management. This is somewhat complicated because new regulations are written, but the old ones will still be in effect and not all countries have the same rules. Some areas of focus for the legitimate business that wants the benefit of the technology while staying firmly above board include:

- AML – Anti- Money Laundering
- KYC – Know Your Customer
- Obligations in tax and accounting

One recent example of how regulators are applying the existing laws to new technologies is a subpoena from the IRS to CoinBase, one of the largest cryptocurrency exchanges in the world.

While Blockchain may have its benefits, the further into the mainstream it goes, the more important risk management will be.

Chapter 4: Blockchain Security Measures

The blockchain is a structure that allows for a digital transactions ledger to be produced and shared over a digital network. The distributed ledger technology is going to enable capital markets and the financial services industry to unlock their full potential in terms of the digital markets by helping them to move on from the inefficient and expensive systems in use today. But just how secure is the blockchain?

It is, in fact, one of the most secure technologies ever created, promising to remove the risks of tampering, cyber crime and fraud and all of this is down to the math beneath the chain, the math that swaddles each transaction in a layer of protection. Distributed ledgers can increase trust because every party in the transaction receives a copy of it. The transaction participants cannot make any changes to the transaction registry; all they can do is add to it and the original transaction is intact and in irreversible. In traditional models, hackers only need to access a database and change a single value to divert the funds; with the blockchain, this cannot be done.

The Chain of Trust

Another one of the major promises of the blockchain exchanges is to establish provenance. Distributed records will establish a complete history of everything in a supply chain. If an issue is found with a specific part, perhaps a dodgy brake pad, the car manufacturers would be able to quickly locate the supplier, the date of manufacture and the production line. This all makes it much easier to narrow down the likelihood of recalls. On top of that, unscrupulous suppliers wouldn't be able to hide anything because they cannot make any changes to that database.

Cyber Security at its Best

The blockchain provides us with an alternative ways of storing data and sharing information, that takes away the single failure points and centralization of traditional methods that can easily be hacked. The technology behind Bitcoin can now be used as a way of beefing up security and preventing cybercrime and it can do this in three ways:

1. **Identity Protection**

One of the commonest forms of encryption used to secure messages, emails, websites and any other communication form online is PKI – Public Key Infrastructure. However, most of the time PKI implementations require trusted, centralized third-party certificate authorities to issue the key pairs, revoke them or store them for every single participant and that gives hackers chance to use them for spoofing identities and cracking encryptions. A recent example is WhatsApp, one of the most popular messaging apps in the world! – it was shown it could be exploited to generate false keys and allow **MITM (man-in-the-middle)** attacks. These are attacks when hackers secretly alter communication with two recipients, but the two parties are not privy to this and believe they have a secured line, but in actual fact it's tampered.

By publishing keys on the blockchain, this risk is eliminated and applications will easily be able to verify the identity of whom you are communicating with. Pomcor, a tech research company, recently published a blueprint for a blockchain that is based on PKI but does not eliminate central authorities. Instead, the blockchain is used for storing hashes of certificates that have been issued or revoked. In this way, users can verify certificate authenticity through a transparent and decentralized source.

2. **Data Integrity**

We use private keys for signing files and documents so that the recipient can verify the data source. Then we go to extraordinary lengths to prove that no tampering has taken place and this is where the problem lies – that key is meant to be private! There is, however, a blockchain alternative and it replaces the private with transparency, distributes the evidence over all the nodes on the network and makes it impossible to manipulate any data without being caught out.

KSI, or Keyless Signature Structure, is a new blockchain project that has one aim – to get rid of key-based authentication. It stores hashes of files and data on the blockchain and verifies copies of that data through hashing algorithms; the results are compared with the original on the blockchain and if anything has been changed, it will swiftly be caught.

The military is already considering KSI for the protection of sensitive data while health care providers are using the blockchain for change-auditing, transparency of data and access-control for health records. This is incredibly important given the amount of sensitive data that is handled by the healthcare providers and the number of times they have been victims of data breaches. The blockchain technology can help them to verify patient data integrity across organizations, create audit trails that cannot be changed and maintain the integrity of clinical trial data.

3. **Critical Infrastructure Protection**

In October, a major DDOS (Distributed Denial of Service) attack taught every one of us how easily hackers can bring critical services to their knees. One single service that provided the DNS for most of the major websites was brought down, cutting off access to Netflix, Twitter, PayPal and many other services for hours. This is just one more example of how centralized infrastructures fail us.

Using the blockchain to store the DNS entries would significantly improve security because it eliminates the one target that a hacker can use to bring the system down. One of the biggest weak points in the current system is caching, which makes it easy for a hacker to stage a DDOS attack against the servers and allows censorship of social media and manipulation of DNS registries by oppressive regimes. None of that will be possible on the blockchain because caching does not exist and because the entire chain is transparent.

A DNS that is distributed and transparent will give owners control of their own records and will stop any person or agency from manipulating the entries as they want to.

The Hyperledger Project

We can't talk about the blockchain without talking about Bitcoin, the poster child for the technology. Bitcoin has been widely shunned by financial institutions because it started life associated with the dark web, because of its lack of accountability and because of its use in ransomware. According to Barclays bank, these financial institutions have a requirement to put measures in place to know their customers and to stop money laundering.

This is why the Hyperledger Project was developed. It is an open-source project that has the support of banks, large manufacturers and insurance companies to address those very real concerns. Features of the Hyperledger include trust insurance, transparency and the ability to use smart contracts. Some of the biggest supporters of the Hyperledger are American Express, London Stock Exchange, JP Morgan Chase & Co and Wells Fargo and one of the tools that has come out of this is something called the Hyperledger Fabric.

Hyperledger was founded in 2015 by the Linux Foundation to advance blockchain technology across industries. Instead of using a single blockchain standard, the project encourages the development of blockchain technologies using a collaborative approach, through a community process and a series of intellectual property rights that will encourage key standard adoption and open development.

Fabric is one of the projects and, like the blockchain, it has the ledger, it makes use of smart contracts and is a system that participants can manage their own transactions in. Where Fabric differs from other blockchains is that it is a private and a permissioned system. Instead of requiring 'proof of work', Fabric members enroll in the network using a membership services provider.

Fabric offers its members:

- The ability to store ledger data in multiple formats
- Consensus mechanisms that may be switched in and out
- Channel creation – groups of participants can create their own separate transactions ledger. This is important where some network participants may not want their competitors to see every transaction they make

Shared Ledgers

The Fabric Ledger subsystem is made up of two components – transaction log and world state. Each of the participants will have a copy of the ledger for each Fabric network they are a member of. World State describes the ledger at any given point and is the ledger database while the transaction log will record every transaction that has resulted in that World State – basically, it is an update history.

Smart Contracts

Smart contracts for Fabric are written using chaincode and these are invoked by blockchain-external applications when there is a need for the application and the ledger to interact. Most of the time, chaincode will only have an interaction with the World State and not the transaction log.

Privacy

Depending on the network requirements, B2B (Business to Business) network participants may well be sensitive about the information that is being shared while for other types of network this may not be such a big concern. Hyperledger Fabric supports those networks that require privacy as an operational requirement as well as those that are open.

Consensus

All transactions must be written to the ledger in the exact order that they happen, although they may not be between the same participants on that network. For this, the transaction order must be established and a method putting in place for rejecting those bad transactions that have been put on the ledger, either in error or for malicious purposes.

Hyper Ledger Fabric was designed to give network starters the option of choosing the best consensus mechanism to suit their needs, retaining privacy, trust, and transparency while being flexible enough to suit all industry types.

Hash Functions & Ledger

What about our names being publically broadcasted on the ledger for public view? No worries, this is solved by something we earlier discussed called a "hash function" which disguises people's identity with a 20 digit unique code (mathematical equation). Masking their real identities and details in a complex arrangement of numbers.

How do we know we are starting from the same transaction version of the record? This can be also addressed by a hash function as well, codes will be compared from computer to computer and if the codes all match it will be verified as accurate. Remember hackers would need to tamper with ledgers from every single computer involved in the transaction to alter information, which is highly unlikely. Making this technology and information of the ledger reliable.

Chapter 5: Bitcoin

Bitcoin is the best and most well-known use of the blockchain and, although blockchain technology is moving onto bigger and better things, Bitcoin will always be the first thing we think of. Bitcoin was the very first and, so far, most successful digital currency. They are created through the act of 'mining' and this involves the use of very expensive hardware to solve mathematical equations. Each 'miner' is rewarded with a Bitcoin or a part of one. The most basic explanation of the Bitcoin is that it is electricity that has been converted into strings of code, each of which has a monetary value.

Why is Bitcoin Controversial?

There are several reasons for this, not least the fact that Bitcoin was used for illegal activities online. From 2011 to 2013, criminal traders purchased batches of Bitcoin costing millions of dollars, purely to get it under the radar and this forced the price of the Bitcoin up. Truthfully though, the real reason why the Bitcoin is so controversial is because it is decentralized; there is no middleman and the power has been taken from the federal banks and given back to the people – and the banks don't like that. Unlike the bank account you hold now, a Bitcoin account cannot be frozen, terminated and it cannot be looked into by the tax man. We also don't need a bank or any other agency to govern Bitcoin – we can do it ourselves.

Although the Bitcoin is a digital or cryptocurrency, as soon as you own them they start to act as physical currency – they have a value and can be traded or used exactly as physical currency. You can buy services or goods with them or you can store them in a digital wallet and hope that the value goes up in time. The wallet is a requirement for buying, using and selling Bitcoin; it is a database, online or offline, that is stored on your computer or another device, or even in the cloud and this is where your coins are kept.

Regulations and Values

The value of a Bitcoin can change daily; sometimes up, sometimes down. Right now, more than millions of Bitcoin are in circulation and the mining continues to dredge up more. However, when the number of Bitcoin in existence reaches 21 million, around about the year 2040, they will stop being created. The Bitcoin is divisible so, when you are purchasing or selling you can do so in bits of a Bitcoin if you wish. The current denominations are:

- Bitcoin = 1,000,000 Bits = 100,000,000 Satoshi
- Bits = 0.0000001 (one-millionth) Bitcoin

- Satoshi = 0.00000001 (one-hundred-millionth) Bitcoin

Bitcoin is not regulated in any way, shape or form. It is a self-contained currency and there is no collateral, like a precious metal, behind it.

How the Bitcoin is Made

A Bitcoin is a data ledger file and is called a blockchain. The blockchain is made up of three components:

- The identifying address – an address generated by your wallet and required for all transactions
- A history – the ledger, showing the history of the coin
- The private key header log – where a digital signature is stored confirming all transactions for the file. These signatures are unique to the user and their wallet.

It is these keys that are the backbone of the Bitcoin security. Each trade is tracked, it is tagged and then it is disclosed publicly. The signatures are confirmed across the network of miners which stops duplicated transactions and forgeries.

An interesting fact worth noting at this point is that, although the digital address of every wallet a Bitcoin touches is recorded, no personal details are, such as name, address or any other identifying detail and this is what makes the system anonymous. And, although your Bitcoin is stored on your device, the history of them is on a public ledger, providing transparency, and deterring the use of Bitcoin for illegal purposes.

Fees

There are no bank fees to pay because no banks are involved. There is, however, a small fee for using Bitcoin. The fees are split between the servers who support the miners, the exchanges that convert the Bitcoin to fiat currency and the mining pools that you may be involved in. These fees are minuscule compared to conventional banking or transfer fees.

Practical Use Cases

1. **Donations -** to non-government approved causes, such as Wikileaks
2. **Purchases -** of goods that the government doesn't approve of. In 2011 for example, the New York State Senator publicly demonstrated how cryptocurrencies were being used to purchase drugs online for home delivery. This resulted in a huge Bitcoin price bubble
3. **Gambling** – there are a lot of online gambling sites that allow users to deposit funds and claim winnings in Bitcoin. The winnings area paid to the same Bitcoin address that deposited the funds, cutting out banks and any other financial agency from the equation.
4. **Purchasing Services** – again, that the government doesn't approve of. A recent example is an Escort site that suddenly found itself unable to make payments for ads through traditional means and turned to Bitcoin. There are also several cam sites that operate only on Bitcoin and other sites that use Bitcoin as a way of gaining privacy and anonymity.
5. **Hiding Assets** – usually in a divorce case and not something you will see much about because of the serious issues it could cause with family. Obviously, this could also be used to hide assets for other reasons, such as bankruptcy and from the government for one reason or another.
6. **Cross-Border Transfers** – Bitcoin is not just used as a way of storing and hiding wealth. One of the most powerful aspects of the blockchain will come when the larger economies rise and/or fall. This is historic and will always happen and this is why there are so many global reserve currencies in the world. Traditionally, gold reserves were used to transfer value but this is not so useful in the digital world. Bitcoin will be the next method of transferring this value across borders.

These are more extreme and out of the way cases, but together with the traditional purchases that you can make with Bitcoin, they all point towards the sheer power that an unregulated, decentralized digital currency can have.

Chapter 6: How the Blockchain is Changing the World

Just lately, blockchain technology has attracted a great deal of attention. As one of the most innovative way of creating contracts and organizing transactions, the blockchain has a real potential to change how we deal with money. The blockchain has been the underlying technology for Bitcoin cryptocurrency since 2008 and there is a good reason why it is such an important technology – it is the only way for secure transactions to be made without interference from a third-party. It is this that makes it a useful technology, not just for cash but for other social organization forms, like voting, work or property.

The name blockchain comes about because each transaction is added to a time-stamped block, each transaction having its own history and each block containing a hash function or key to the next block, thus joining it together. This blockchain technology is representing nothing less than a regeneration of the internet and it has the potential to transform everything, from money to business, from governments to society.

Think about this – when you send something over the internet to another person, be it an email, a PDF or .DOC file, or a JPG you are not sending them the original, merely a copy. Depending on what rights the recipients have, they might be able to print the copy but you cannot print money. For that, we must put our trust in a series of powerful middlemen like banks, and governments. These banks and governments, even social media sites to a certain extent, work hard to establish who we are and our asset ownership. In short, they assist us in settling transactions and transferring value.

They don't do a bad job but they do have their limitations. They make use of central servers – these can be hacked into. They charge fees for what they do, sometimes high fees like 10% of the value of a transfer to another country for example. They hold on to our data, undermining what privacy we have. They are not always reliable and most certainly are not always fast at what they do. They also cut out more than 2 billion people who have insufficient means to open a bank account.

This is where the blockchain steps in and takes over, the first ever digital medium for full P2P value exchange, Distributed computations and a real heavy-duty encryption system ensure the integrity of all the data that is traded over millions of different devices without ever going through any third-party. The trust has been hard-coded into the blockchain platform and therefore it is called the Trust Protocol. The blockchain is an accounts ledger, it is a database, a sentry, a notary and it is a clearinghouse, all rolled into one and all by consensus.

But why would you care about this? What difference will it mean to you? Perhaps you love music and you want artists to be able to earn a living from their music. Perhaps you are an aid worker and to rebuild homes after a natural disaster you need to be able to identify homeowners. Maybe you are a public citizen who has had enough of politicians not being transparent or accountable. It doesn't really matter what you are or who you are; someone, somewhere is, right now, building applications based on blockchain technology that will serve your purpose and these are only the tip of the iceberg.

Every single business, every government, agency, and individual can get some benefit from the blockchain. Let's face it, it is already causing severe disruption to the financial services industry. The internet of things, all those devices connected, sending and receiving data, generating their own power, trading it, the ones that protect the environment, help us to manage our health and our homes – this internet of things will eventually require a ledger of everything!

Social inequality is on the rise the poor keep getting poorer and the rich keep exponentially increasing their wealth. The gap continuously grows between the two and, by using the blockchain we can change; no longer will we distribute wealth, we will distribute opportunity and value on a fair basis. Yes, there will be winners and there will be losers, but, so long as we do this right, the blockchain can be the beginning of a new era and age of prosperity for everyone.

4 Unexpected Ways the Blockchain Could Change the World

1. Distributed Cloud Storage

Already, the blockchain has undergone some change to improve security measures so that information can be stored in a way that is unscaleable. As well as being something of a techie hobby, the storage of data on the blockchain could also be seen as disruptive. Right now, cloud storage services are all centralized, meaning a user places their trust into one provider. The blockchain will decentralize this. Take Stori for example, which is a cloud storage facility currently in beta. It uses a network powered by the blockchain to improve security and reduce dependency. Users can rent out any extra storage capacity they have, enabling the traditional cloud to be stored more than 300 times over. Cloud storage currently costs the world $22 billion a year and the ability to rent excess space will do two things – provide a revenue stream for some users and cut the cost of cloud data storage to personal and business users.

2. Contracts That Cannot Be Broken

A smart contract is one that is self-executing or self-enforcing. The role that the blockchain plays in these contracts is to take the place of the third-party that is normally needed to resolve legal disputes. Tokens, otherwise known as 'colored coins' or 'smart properties' may be used as representatives of asset and the ability to hard-code the ownership transfer when you trade the assets can create what we call 'unbreakable' contracts.

Take a widget factory, for example. They currently produce red widgets only, but they get an order from a brand-new customer, for 100 blue widgets. The factory now has to purchase new machinery to service this order and the only way they could possibly get their investment back is for the customer to go through with the order.

In the traditional world, the factory would trust the customer to pay or they would hire a lawyer to enforce the contract – this costs mega-bucks. With the blockchain, they can create a smart property that has a self-executing contract – this contract could say that for every widget delivered, a specific price per item is taken from the customer's bank account and out in the factory account. This does two things – cuts out the need for a deposit or the use of an escrow account, which uses a third-party, and it protects the customer by stopping the factory from not delivering or under delivering.

Right now, this is mostly just theory but already Ethereum platform is pulling the smart contract closer to being a reality.

3. **No More Patents**

In the same way as the Smart Contract platforms, (PoE) ProofOfExistence.com has already launched a series of basic legal services that can be used. This is one of the first recorded uses of the blockchain that is not financial in nature. PoE will store information that is encrypted on the blockchain, recording a transaction hash which cannot be replaced and is associated with a document that is not stored on the blockchain.

The obvious case for this is patents. Let's say Samsung or Apple wanted to prove that they created a specific technology on a specific date but they don't want to file for a public patent. Using the blockchain, the company could prove that ownership by revealing documents that are linked to a specific hash which will show on a specific date on the blockchain.

4. **Electronic Voting**

The current method of having to count every paper and postal vote for an election is becoming archaic, costly in terms of time, money and on accuracy. It is a method that is full of technical issues, such as the accuracy of a machine during a recount cannot be verified and those machines are also huge targets for hackers. In some countries, the blockchain is now being used by political parties for internal voting.

Each transaction on a blockchain contains a hash that verifies the succeeding hash and, in terms of voting, this would mean that, if one vote were changed, millions of other would need to be changed before another can be cast. The blockchain network is protected simply because there is no hacker alive who has sufficient computing power to do this in such a short space of a time.

Also, because of the anonymity factor, each of the votes can be shared publicly without the voter being identified in any way. In this way, every voter can ensure that their vote has been counted and, one day, the blockchain could signal the end of voting and election corruption.

Blockchain technology has got, potentially, millions of different applications and, while most are still in preliminary development stages now, they will eventually make their way into your life, one way or another. In the future, instead of saying, "look it up on Google", the new buzz phrase is likely to be "check it on blockchain."

Prediction: Changing The World In Many Ways

Banks - Blockhain technology will enable almost everyone around the world, even people living in third world countries to have the means of financial access via bitcoin (BTC). -BTC uses fundamental blockchain technology to function.

Cyber Security - Although blockchain is accessible to the public it uses complex math and cryptography to enhance security, thus making it extremely difficult for anyone to hack and tamper with it.

Supply Chain Management - All transactions are permanently recorded in sequential order from point of begging to end, and constantly monitored through general consensus among the blockchain network for accuracy and authenticity purposes.- Increasing efficiency, reducing errors and time delays.

Insurance - Insurance is based on the principal of trust management, blockchain can be used to accurately verify data, such as insured person's identity, residence, etc. The chances for fraud is extremely slim as you know blockchain has state of the art advanced security measures.

Transportation - We've all heard of Uber? Well now blockchain is looking to create decentralized peer to peer ride sharing apps, ways for car owners and users to establish terms and conditions of transportation without third party intermediaries (Uber).

Charity - Common issues with charities are corruption and inefficiencies. Blockchain technology will ensure transparent record keeping and create a permanent sequential, tamper resistant record to track, so there are no chances of money scandals or frauds we always hear about in the news. Ensuring only the intended recipient receives the funds.

Voting - Voting scandals and rigging can happen anywhere in the world, and even here in the west we are not immune to scandals, remember the 2016 US election? It's not the first time political parties have been accused for rigging results. Blockchain technology can be utilized for voter registration and identity confirmation , and also electronic vote counting would ensure only legitimate votes are counted.

No votes could be taken away or added, thus creating an indisputable publically accessible ledger. How's that for democracy?

Governments - Government system are often slow, ambiguous and extremely frustrating. Implementing blockchain based systems will decrease bureaucracy, increase efficiency and uphold transparency.

Health Care - Secure storage platforms for information utilizing blockchain technology will enhance security and prevent hacking. Safely storing data such as medical records and sharing it only with the intended recipient. Improving data security and possibly even speed up diagnosis.

Energy Management - This has been a centralized monopoly for the longest time. But with blockchain technology you would be able to buy forms of energy, ie : electricity in a peer to peer fashion, thus electricity producers and users could buy directly from each other on a decentralized system. Currently we have to use trusted private intermediaries.

Online Music - Blockchain technology is working on a way to pay musicians and artists directly, instead of forfeiting large chunks of royalties to platforms or record labels. Artists/musicians would be able to keep more of the their profits!

Retail - Connecting buyers and sellers without additional fees. Exchanging in commerce without middlemen or intermediaries. In this case blockchain technology would use smart contract systems, and built in reputation management systems.

Real Estate - Eliminate the archaic paper based record keeping system, fraud, and uphold transparency. Blockchain would ensure ownership, accuracy, and even transferring property deeds.

Crowd Funding - A lot of companies use crowd funding platforms, however often times these platforms charge high fees. Blockchain could eliminate these fees by implementing smart contracts and online reputation based systems. New projects would release funds by generating their own "tokens" that have an associated value, and later be exchanged for products, services or cash.

Merkel Tree

In cryptography a "merkel tree" refers to all transactions of a block that are hashed together forming tree like pattern, until a merkel root is reached. (full explanation next page)

Diagram Below:

ABCD (Merkel Root)

^(Branch**)**

AB   **CD**

A **^** B   C **^** D

Breakdown: A & B = **AB** ,   C & D = **CD** ,   AB & CD = **ABCD**

Merkel Tree Details :

By now you have looked at the merkel tree diagram and are probably wondering what it all means? The merkel tree is considered a data structure I'll elaborate, the bottom 4 values "$A \wedge B$" & "$C \wedge D$" are hashed together with a branch (^).

Hash = ^

Now imagine each one of these values represents a transaction in a block (A,B,C,D). In order for all the nodes to validate the transactions, this would require a large amount of computation resources and storage. If we had a mobile app that utilized blockchain it wouldn't be realistic to send all these transactions to the app. Thus, we need a way to validate the transaction without sending all of them at once.

So how do we arrive to a solution? Well, we simply hash them together as previously mentioned:

We hash $A \wedge B$ creating a totally new value **"AB"**. Ergo, $A \wedge B = AB$

The same exact process is followed for **C & D**. We hash **$C \wedge D$** together. Therefore, **$C \wedge D$** = "**CD**". Again we create a totally unique and new value.

Lastly we hash **AB** & **CD** together: **AB** ^**CD** = **"ABCD"**

ABCD is the" merkel root". As you can see it is the last blockchain in the series of hashes that connect to it.

Now if we are to change any single piece of these values of A,B,C,D, than the entire merkel root value would change as a result. So when one value alters this in turn changes all the other values as well. For example if you were to change the initial values at the bottom of the merkel tree to **A^X** than the **merkel root** would become **"AXCD".**

Do you see the beauty of the merkel tree? This enables blockchain to be tamper resistant and extremely difficult to cheat. So for example, if a client wanted to validate value "A", what would happen is a computer would use the merkel root "ABCD" and the prior values to validate if in fact value "A" exists on the data structure of the merkel tree.

The merkel root validates the prior sequences in a transaction. Ergo, it is nearly impossible to scam, con or cheat the blockchain system. Usually, you only need the merkel root in order to validate any given value. Since "A" is found in the merkel root it is therefore successfully validated as an accurate value. Let's say, someone tried to change a value, for example purposes lets use "Z". Well than the blockchain system would check the merkel root "ABCD", and since "Z" is not found within this merkel root it is denied and not an accepted value.

Summary

The widespread adoption of blockchain technology is inevitable. When it comes to money people have to place their trust in a third party, whether money, services, goods, etc. However, blockchain technology utilizes math and cryptography providing an open data base that is decentralized, meaning no one has ownership over this system unlike current standards and practices we live with today. Establishing a permanent record that can be verified by the community.

Since the dawn of civilization people have always recorded transactions between the exchange of goods and services on stone tablets and paper. We now have evolved proportionate to the growth of commerce worldwide, and documenting such tasks has become quite complex with various methodologies of documentation, which in a lot of cases gives room for error, fraud and mistakes!

Example

Gold is a precious commodity we used today. This is a prime example of how blockchain technology will enhance security, transparency, efficiency and satisfaction between all parties. Let me elaborate how blockchain will impact this historically treasured rock in a positive manner.

The gold industry has to go through a complex framework consisting of legal, regulatory, financial, manufacturing and other commercial practices. This consists of various intermediaries, lawyers, accountants, banks and legal officials. Current methods posses vulnerabilities and are susceptible to counterfeit gold, corruption and unethically derived gold. As you can see the current arduous process is time consuming and adds to overall cost.

(Gold Mines ---> Manufacturing---> Regulatory bodies --> Financial Institutions ---> Lawyers & Legal Officials --> Accountants --->Jewelers --> Sold to Customer.)

Now this is where blockchain comes in and its advanced technology shines, I'll explain, blockchain uses a open source data base, in essence a publicly accessed and authenticated ledger. Blockchain offers all parties involved in the transaction a secure, synchronized and updated sequence of records from point of origins to end. Meaning every single sequence of transaction that occurs is shown on this ledger, ergo creating an irreversible chain of blocks linked together sequentially from beginning to end.

That's why blockchain is favorable and very applicable for implementation in practical everyday use in the world we live in. Imagine being able to find out the origins of an item your purchasing with pinpoint accuracy, transparency and clarity, and not worry about anything unethical surrounding it.

Blockchain: 3 Tamper Resistant Security Features

1.Distributed

Distributed means everyone gets a copy of the ledger meaning there is no "one" centralized system that has ownership of records. -This eliminates any possibilities of tampering with or altering of information. This functions as a shared form of record keeping ensuring no one entity or organization is only privy to it.

2.Authenticated

When an item cycles through the transaction chain, for example gold, everyone not only has access to that information from the ledger, but also authenticates the information through the means of a general consensus among the blockchain network. Information recorded in the blockchain is permanent meaning no one can add to or take away from it, without the consensus of everyone on the network.

3.Secure

Continuing with the example gold, at the end of a transaction cycle certificates of authenticity, real time records, payment transactions, and even product details are provided. As you can see there is a complete auditable and irrefutable record of information accessible to everyone involved in the transaction cycle.

This will make life so much easier for people worldwide. This will eliminate barriers that people have in third world countries and enable their inclusion. This will make sending money back home easier for immigrants where access to financial institutions is limited. Perhaps in the future near blockchain technology will be implemented to collect taxes within countries this way nobody would be able to evade taxes.

The opportunities are boundless and the world is forever changing, what will blockchain technology change next?

Conclusion

Thank you for taking the time to read my book and I truly hope that you now have a much better understanding of the blockchain and what makes it tick. As I said earlier, the blockchain is not simple and it is quite complex. But once you do understand it, you can easily see the benefits of it, not just for you but for the future of finance, for the future of every transaction, be it money, goods or services.

You have seen how Bitcoin works, the single biggest use of the blockchain to date but blockchain technology is leaving Bitcoin behind. It is moving on in leaps and bounds, finding new uses and applications every day, and will eventually become the standard by which we all live by. Centralized agencies, like banks, credit agencies, even governments are fast losing the trust of the people; the fact that they are constantly monitoring every move we make, and always giving us the short end of the stick.

People want to stay anonymous but they want to be safe and secure at the same time. While Bitcoin first started out as a method of money laundering and other criminal activities, it has long moved on and the blockchain is now clean; although many banks and governments still don't trust it because its nefarious start, they are beginning to see the light and they are beginning to see how they can put the blockchain to use to clean up their own acts, to make every transaction accountable and transparent.

As you have seen, the cryptography that secures blockchain technology is complex; having seen how the public and private keys work, you can see how encryption works to keep you safe, to stop the blockchain from being hacked and misused. You can see how hard it is for someone to change any transaction for their own benefit and you can see how any errors are picked up and stopped in their tracks immediately if they happen.

Lastly, you have seen what the blockchain does now and what it can be used for in the real world. This really is only the tiny tip of a very large iceberg; blockchain technology is changing the world as we know it and, as time goes by, more services, more governments, and financial institutions are going to jump on the bandwagon and implement blockchain technologies for various practical applications.

It is time for the world to become accountable for every transaction made, from the smallest purchase right up to major international transactions carried out by government agencies. Blockchain technology is here to stay and is one innovation that the world will not be able to live without in years to come; it is an innovation that has caused a major upset amongst world powers and governments and it will continue to do so for the foreseeable future.

It's time for the future to become transparent, accountable and secure. It's time for the hackers and malicious users to be pushed out, leaving us safe in the knowledge that our money is secure.

We need to embrace change, encourage innovation , and nurture creativity in order to secure a bright and boundless future for generations to come.

You've reach the end. Congrats.

If you enjoyed this book can you leave a quality review on Amazon please see link below..

LINK: http://amzn.to/2sQKeyM

Other books written by Raymond Kazuya

Bitcoin & Cryptocurrencies Guide: Introduction Learn Everything You Need To Know!

LINK: : http://amzn.to/2tRQpyj

LINK: Investing in Etherum Cryptocurrencies & Profiting Guide

http://amzn.to/2uuGVt9

GLOSSARY

Merkel Tree - A data structure made up of hashes, blockchain, and merkel root. Enabling efficient and secure authentication for transactions, especially large transactions.

Hash - Branch (^) that connects values together and creates a totally unique and new value from the previous existing values. Basically a hash functions serves to takes some input data and creates some output data. It takes the input of any length to create an output of a fixed length.

Cryptography - The practice and study of techniques in secure communication. In essence deciphering codes that have intended messages.

Smart Contracts - procedures that mediate, validate and negotiate performance of a contract.

Hyper Ledger - An open record data base accessible to anyone in the public that verifies the authenticity of a transaction.

Consensus - Agreement among nodes or blockchain networks which validate a transaction.

Logarithms - is the inverse operation to exponentiation. It's like how division is the inverse of multiplication. For example the base of 10 logarithm of 1000 is 3, meaning 10 to the power of 3. Therefore, 10 is used as a factor 3 times.

Algorithms - set of rules that are used to perform complex calculations, usually conducted by a computer.

Encryption - Converting data into a complex code, thus concealing data from unauthorized access.

Authenticate - The process of validating the accuracy of a transaction. Confirming if certain values within a transaction is legitimate or not.

Bitcoin - An intangible cryptocurrency that is used like any other fiat currency to purchase or exchange goods and services. We ascribe value to Bitcoins much like we do the USD or EU.

Diagrams

How the bitcoin exchange process works see below:

Bitcoin
↓
BTC network
↓
Authentication Process
↓
Validation through the Ledger
↓
Consensus via BTC Network
↓
Miners Paid as an Incentive

INVESTING IN ETHEREUM CRYPTOCURRENCIES & PROFITING: GUIDE

RAYMOND KAZUYA

Investing In Ethereum Cryptocurrencies & Profiting Guide

Table of Contents

Introduction

10 years ago, digital currency was almost unheard of except in small, elite circles. Today, all we hear are words like "cryptocurrency," "Bitcoin," "Blockchain" and now new ones, "Ethereum" and "smart contracts." All these words and more are fast becoming part of everyday language, no matter where you are in the world and, while most people now have a better understanding of them, especially Bitcoin, Ethereum remains something of a mystery to most people.

Ethereum is the world's first platform that will allow us to run applications in a way that is trustless, uncensorable and unstoppable – the three qualities that make cryptocurrencies so popular. All three of these qualities can be taken and applied to just about any application you could possibly think of. Smart contracts are the future of the world as we know it, contracts that will run automatically without the need for intermediaries and without the need for worry about whether they can be fulfilled or not.

Bitcoin started slowly and built up a head of steam that just keeps on billowing out and many people believe that Ethereum is just the next Bitcoin. It isn't; it is so much more than that. Ethereum is the future, second to Bitcoin only in terms of the volumes of transactions carried out on it. It has grown exponentially faster than Bitcoin in a much shorter period and some of that may be attributed to Bitcoin boosting confidence and excitement levels in digital currencies, but Ethereum stands apart from all the others.

Bitcoin was complicated; you needed to have an understanding of cryptography and a lot of disposable income that you could spend on the equipment needed to mine it. Ethereum changes all that and makes using the blockchain easy, putting it in within reach of Joe Public. It gives more people more chances to make more money.

It's time to learn what Ethereum can do for you and how it's more than just a blockchain currency. Ethereum is the Queen to the Bitcoin King; the Silver to the Bitcoin Gold but it has the potential to take the crown in both. Ethereum is a digital asset, one that could be one of the greatest investments you have ever made. Indeed, Ethereum is better suited to investment than Bitcoin ever was, simply because it is easier to make money with it without spending a fortune on it.

In this guide, you will learn:

- What Ethereum is
- How it works
- What Smart Contracts are
- All about Ethereum mining
- How to invest in Ethereum
- How it is used already in the world today
- Where it is heading in the future

You may be surprised to learn that there are already dozens of major organizations that use Ethereum and smart contracts. You may be even more surprised to learn that investing in Ethereum is not difficult and anyone can do it – I will show you how to do it - although, as with any investment - you do need to understand that there is a risk involved. That's the nature of investing and, as long as you understand that from the beginning, there is no reason why you can't make some serious money.

Right now, the price of Ethereum is rising fast and it is now one of the most promising and most sought-after cryptocurrencies in the world. Want to learn more? Read on to discover everything you need to know about Ethereum.

Chapter 1: What is Ethereum?

If you have been following the financial news or the tech news, no doubt you have seen and heard the word "Ethereum." Normally, you will have heard it in connection with Bitcoin but the two are not be confused. Ethereum is one of the fastest growing cryptocurrencies in the world but, strictly speaking, Ethereum isn't a cryptocurrency as such.

It is actually a platform that lets developers build decentralize applications, conduct transactions and draw up smart contracts. This is all done with a currency known as Ether, another form of the cryptocurrency that does not have a physical form and is created entirely through encryption. It is nothing more than data on a digital ledger, a ledger that we all know of as the blockchain. This blockchain is shared far and wide publicly, on every computer that has the right software on it. Whenever a transaction takes place, it is added to a block and that block is validated by some of the computers on the network. The most crucial part of this, the part that ensures transactions cannot be tampered with, is that the ledger is shared in its entirety, every time a new transaction happens, with all network computers, or nodes as they are called. Anyone can see this ledger and can track every single Ethereum transaction that has ever happened – if anyone tried to make any changes, everyone would be able to see it.

The transactions are validated by miners and this is done through the solving of highly complex mathematical equations. I will be talking more about mining in a later chapter but, suffice to say, for now, it is intensive. The miners are rewarded for validating the blocks with a payment of a certain amount of Ether.

When a transaction is carried out using a cryptocurrency, the transaction is authenticated by a digital signature. This is created through two cryptography keys. The first is a public key, which is your Ethereum "address" and, whenever you are sent Ether, it is sent to that address. When you send Ether to someone else, a private key is used. This is a kind of password, randomly generated, that gives you the authority to carry out a transaction with the Ether, generating a message that creates the digital signature. This signature is then used by the miners to verify the transaction. Each new transaction has a unique signature, generated each time, stopping transactions from being repeated.

Why is this so important?

In the past, digital transactions have always needed a third-party like a bank, to authorize that transaction and validate it. Digital money is, at its most basic, a file which

may be copied and then reused but these intermediaries are not free – every bank and every authority requires everyone else to pay the fees they demand for letting them play in their sandbox.

The idea behind cryptocurrencies is to get around these authorities but transactions still need to be tracked to stop double-spending. Let's face it, if anyone could just go and create a copy of the digital currency they hold, and keep on spending it over and over, the currency would become next to useless.

The blockchain allows P2P (peer to peer) transactions without the need for that third party. They are secure by nature because nothing can be tampered with or changed without everybody on the network seeing it and having to revalidate the transaction.

All of this applies to Ethereum in the same way that it does to Bitcoin but both have completely different goals. Bitcoin is ONLY a digital currency, designed as a way of making payment for a service or goods, whereas Ethereum goes much further – it is a platform that allows the use of tokens to create applications, run them and, perhaps, more importantly, the ability to create smart contracts.

What is a smart contract?

A smart contract is a piece of code that will run when conditions that are specifically defined are met. The uses of a smart contract are virtually limitless, especially where the result required is exchange. Many companies are now using these smart contracts in the supply chain to ensure the quality of their products and the dispatch of them.

A smart contract is a contract that has been written in computer code and uploaded by the creator to the blockchain. Whenever a contract is executed, every computer on the network runs it because it is stored on the blockchain and is, in theory, tamper-proof.

If you understand computer programming, you will understand me when I say that a smart contract is a structured if...then statement. Provided specific conditions are met, the terms of the contract will be carried out. An example would be if you wanted to rent a vehicle and the company uses Ethereum. A smart contract would be drawn up and generated – the condition would be that you send a specified amount of funds. When that is met, a digital key is sent to you so that you can unlock the car.

This is all done on the blockchain so that when the Ether tokens are sent the whole network sees what has happened. In the same way, that network can also see that the key has been sent to you. Another condition could be added to this contract - one that says if the key is not sent to you then your tokens will be refunded. This transaction cannot be tampered with because everyone can see it.

Each program that is on Ethereum needs to use a certain amount of processing power and because this is all run by the network nodes, superfluous activities need to be kept to an absolute minimum. Because of this, every program and every contract on Ethereum is provided with a cost of gas. This is a measurement of the amount of processing power needed for the contract or program – the higher the requirement in gas, the more it will cost the user in Ether tokens.

The smart contract effectively removes the need for intermediaries like banks, notaries or lawyers which mean no fees to pay and this is important for those who reside in countries where the legal system is inefficient or downright corrupt. One downside to this is that if something went wrong such as a bug in the coding, the contract terms would still be carried out and this could cause problems.

That said, things are improving all the time and work on Ethereum is ongoing. It is still one of the safest ways to carry out a transaction and set up a contract.

Chapter 2: Ethereum vs Bitcoin vs Litecoin

There is no doubt that Bitcoin remains the largest cryptocurrency in the world but Ethereum is snapping hard at its heels. While the two do function similarly, they are designed and structured in very different ways. Where Bitcoin is a blockchain-based currency, allowing for the safe and anonymous transfer of funds with no regulation or centralized authority, Ethereum has borrowed the blockchain but expanded it for much more than just a payment method.

Currency vs Computer

The blockchain technology needs a very large distributed network to function, a transaction ledger where every single transaction gets recorded on every point of the network. This gives users the ability to send and receive the currency without a bank overseeing every move they make and charging well for the privilege.

Ethereum and Bitcoin are both based on this blockchain but Ethereum can do so much more and can accept much more advanced commands. This is because it has added a Turing-complete language to all interactions on the blockchain. This is what enables the smart contracts to be created. You could say that Ethereum is a virtual computer, built out of nodes on the blockchain and with each command having to be confirmed by the whole computer and saved to the ledger.

Bitcoin blocks hold transaction information but Ethereum blocks hold much more, with the ability to function as a completely autonomous contract. Put simply, instead of sending money to a specified account, Ether can be used to create a contract that completes as soon as conditions are met. This contract is verified, validated and put on the Ethereum blockchain, not moving until all terms have been met and the contract is complete.

What about mining?

Bitcoin mining requires the use of specialized hardware and, for a single user, is not likely to be profitable given the cost of the equipment and the energy required to carry out the mining. With Ethereum, however, a different system is in place, favoring those users with home computers rather than expensive gear that goes out of date very quickly. This is to encourage a much stronger network and more independent miners. That said, like Bitcoin, investment is required to earn money from Ethereum, just not as much as Bitcoin requires.

In both Ethereum and Bitcoin, miners make use of the computer power to solve the problems, known as 'proof of work' problems, resulting in the block of information being added to the blockchain. Both sets of miners are rewarded for mining each block and are paid in either Bitcoin or Ether.

Because the Bitcoin blockchain has a limited block size, each transfer can take an hour or more to be confirmed while transactions on Ethereum take, on average, about three minutes. The transaction fee that is paid to the miners has another use in Ethereum – it stops users from carrying out spam or other attacks against smart contracts and this is because of the high cost of large-volume transactions. Transaction fees on both are kept to a minimum.

Bitcoin mining for profit and investment is an extremely competitive field and in order to do so you have to follow some steps to ensure you can mine safely and profitably.

If you are a professional coder and have experience Linux or Ubuntu, then you may feel that your mining experience may be enhanced by using an established platform such as Genesis. Genesis mining is one of the leading cloud mining companies and provides the best option for smart ways to invest.

Join the team of experts and take advantage of the bitcoin mining algorithm that has been designed to provide rentals that can be used to mine in an efficient and reliable way.

Chances are you are more interested in a way for the individual with limited experience to enter the field of bitcoin mining.

It has to be pointed out that in the past mining could be done with an ordinary computer, but as the niche has become so competitive you will need to use ASIC miners, that's application specific integrated circuit to you and me, in order to mine successfully.

Details of how you can obtain this hardware are available on the internet and you should be able to pick up what you need.

Firstly, we must ascertain if the process of bitcoin mining is even capable of producing a profit when applied to your circumstances. This can be worked out with a bitcoin mining calculator.

Once you have your mining calculator on your screen you will need to enter your mining hardware hash rate in GH/s, your power wattage and the cost of your electricity in dollars per Kw per hour. The calculator will automatically insert the level of difficulty, block reward and current bitcoin price.

Once the data has been entered you will receive a number of sets of figures. The calculations will be as follows

4. How many days it will take to generate one block of BTC with solo mining

5. How many days to generate a single bitcoin

6. How many days will it take to not see a loss

It is worth noting that all of these figures can vary greatly depending on exchange rates and sometimes just old-fashioned luck! These figures should also be taken as a guideline and should not be used to invest money. Any money used to invest in mining must be classed as "spare cash" due to the uncertainty and various variables that applies to the process.

You have now done your calculations and have decided you want to take this route. Time to choose your miner. There is plenty of material in the form of hardware reviews that can be used to help you make an informed choice.

Before we go any further a bitcoin wallet is needed, a fairly straightforward process. If you visit Bitcoin's site there are a host of alternative to choose from. In order to use your wallet for mining you will need to know your public address and not your private key.

Now we need to find a mining pool. It is not advised to mine individually as it is very unlikely that you will come across a bitcoin block and since that is how the currency is awarded, usually in a block of 12.5 at a time you will have more success when working as a group.

Choosing your pool is a very important part of the process. Below are the considerations that you must consider when choosing your pool.

6. Pool fee: Many consider this to be the main consideration when choosing your pool. Normally the fees range from 0% to 4% and the standard fee is generally 1%. If you find a pool that has the same features as another but a lower fee then choose that one but keep an eye on the fee structure.

    a. It is also possible to find a pool that has a 0% fee, unusual but not unheard of. This would normally indicate a new pool that is looking to attract customers. Again, keep an eye on fee structures.

7. Payment system: General rule of thumb is determined by risk. If the pool operator is assuming the risk then it follows that they will pay a lower rate than a pool in which the miners assume the risk. This can also affect fee structure. Your first decision is to either accept a greater percentage of risk, pay less fees but accept that you may create less income. Alternatively, you could join a pool that guarantees a lower rate of profit but the pool operator guarantees payment for every proof of work.

8. Minimum payout: When choosing a pool, you will need to check out the payout period, the minimum payout and who is responsible for transaction fees. By determining if it is the pool or the user who pays fees you can make informed choices.

9. Currency: Choosing the mining currency you wish to mine is a consideration you will need to address. Currently there are a number of alternatives. If you want to

mix it up a little the multi-pool option may appeal to you. These allow mining of several crypto currencies at any time and can convert your profits into BTC once you decide to withdraw funds.

10. Geography: Always check your pool has servers in your country, or at least your continent! If they do check the URL for the servers and choose the one that allows you to mine more efficiently.

You will now need to get a mining program for your computer. If you have chosen a pool that already uses software like BitMinter then you are good to go. If, however the pool you have joined does not have its own software then you will need to choose your own.

Compare different mining software by checking the internet, two of the most popular programs are BFG miner and 50Miner.

All ready to go mining? Then let's begin! Connect your miner to the power and then attach it to your computer with a USB lead. Once you have opened up your mining software you will need to join your pool and enter your user name and password.

Once this is done you will begin mining for bitcoins, or your other chosen cryptocurrencies.

The actual process of mining is essentially releasing blocks of BTC by solving complex mathematical problems and algorithms. While there are millions of these equations surrounding each block of BTC not all of the equations have to be solved to release the block. This is where "chance" comes into play. You could unlock a block of BTC on the first, the hundredth or the millionth time you solve a problem.

The key is to find the winning equation that releases the block. How fast the problems are solved is determined by the speed and power of the computer solving it.

As a user, you are simply telling your computer that you want to mine, that is what the mining software is for, and at any one time there are tens of thousands of computers working on each equation at the same time and looking to release the same block of BTC. Therefore, it is suggested that you join a mining pool as opposed to working alone.

There has been four generations of mining hardware and modern miners are most likely to have dedicated mining rigs that are solely for the purpose of mining bitcoin.

Will there be a future without bitcoin mining? Simple answer- yes there will. It is believed that the final bitcoin will be produced by 2140 and as the final blocks are released there will be no more to reveal. Until then the number of people trying to mine currency grows every day and the chances of making a profit by this method becomes more difficult but that is the chance you take.

Bitcoin mining is a gamble, you will need to weigh up the pros and cons, examine the startup costs and decide if this is the route you want to take. If it is then happy mining and may your hard work bring you profit!!

Not your thing? Maybe you will be content simply buying currency and waiting for the price to rise. Whatever you decide then make sure you check out all information thoroughly.

Value and Decentralization

Both currencies are decentralized but Ethereum encourages users to mine with consumer graphic cards to prevent 51% attacks and collusion. The blockchain nodes for Bitcoin are grouped into pools and some of these pools control a high percentage of all the blocks that are mined. This leads to a higher risk of collusion.

Proof-of-work was the first solution that came out to protect the security of the blockchain. Ethereum developers have come up with a new way, one that increases decentralization even further and results in a lower cost with regards to computer

power. It's called a Proof-of-Stake system and it takes the place of mining with a system of staking the currency on whether or block can or should be put onto the blockchain.

Both Bitcoin and Ethereum are, by far the biggest cryptocurrencies on the market but, despite the volatility of both, Bitcoin has managed to keep its lead by a nose, as well as being the highest value cryptocurrency available right now. But what about other cryptocurrencies? How do they compare to Ethereum?

Ethereum vs Litecoin

Up until just recently, Litecoin was second to Bitcoin until it was firmly displaced by Ethereum. Comparing the two is like comparing a carrot with a beetroot. They may both be vegetables but that is where the similarity ends. Litecoin was originally released in 2011, as a way of overcoming challenges in Bitcoin mining. Litecoin mining times were shorter and where Bitcoin has a limit of 21 million coins, Litecoin went above and beyond this, aiming for a cap at 84 million tokens.

In terms of similarity, Ethereum and Litecoin are miles apart. Where Litecoin attempted to take over from Bitcoin, so Ethereum was slated to topple Litecoin, being released for a much bigger purpose than just mining and creating coins for transactions. Ether, the Ethereum currency, is created mainly to facilitate an exchange of value for services that are carried out on the platform. This platform is an immense decentralized computer powered by millions of other computers like the Bitcoin blockchain is. The core development team behind Ethereum have taken the necessary steps to stop the platform from being misused, purely for creating currency hand over fist, like they do on Litecoin and Bitcoin.

Litecoin also uses the Proof-of Work mining system that Bitcoin uses, again, different to the Proof-of-Stake algorithm used by Ethereum miners. It is this system that stops monopolization of the platform, as has happened with other cryptocurrencies – we have seen occurrences of both Litecoin and Bitcoin mining being taken over by large organizations with the money to purchase the most expensive equipment and fill up entire warehouses with it, effectively stopping the at-home miner from being able to compete. Proof-of-Stake makes it possible for everyone to be equal and it places a limit

on what functions may be performed on the Ethereum platform, simply through how much Ether each user possesses.

In short, Ethereum is a computational platform where Bitcoin and Litecoin are transactional systems. The currency is Ether and this is required for users to use any of the memory and processing power provided by the Ethereum protocol. Those who contribute get a reward of Ether and they can use this to build and host applications or trade it in for another type of cryptocurrency.

Litecoin, like Bitcoin, is a monetary platform, faster than Bitcoin and a good deal more efficient but, like Bitcoin, it has become a platform for those with the ability to invest serious money in mining, locking out the average user. It is highly unlikely that Litecoin will ever take back its crown as the second cryptocurrency and may even end up falling further as Ethereum continues to rise through the ranks.

Chapter 3: Real World Use of Ethereum

2016 proved to be very productive in terms of blockchain technology research and interest in it has resulted in several applications in industries across the world already. However, the blockchain isn't all that is turning heads.

Ethereum has introduced the smart contract, allowing for the automation of tasks that would normally require the intervention of third-parties thus promoting fewer oversight issues and less reliance on trust agents. It is the smart contract that has turned Ethereum into one of the most innovative platforms that could revolutionize different industries, in different ways.

Prediction and Financial Services Markets

In the near future, the financial services sector is going to expand rather quickly. Platforms, such as Branche, are planning to cause disruption to the industry through the introduction of Ethereum blockchain solutions for basic services like check cashing and Microcredit. As well as that, investors have also been given the opportunity to use a decentralized platform called ICONOMI, which is looking to give those investors the tools they need to return a decent profit in an economy that is decentralized.

A decentralized prediction market called Augur is a tool that predicts real-world events and it allows users to make a prediction on something that is happening right now and potentially make a profit if they are correct.

Real Estate

Several Ethereum projects are looking to cause disruption to the real estate market through the implementation of smart contracts. These contracts will cut down on the amount of friction caused by liens, payments and mortgage contracts. These smart contracts will also help to eliminate concerns about privacy between borrowers and lenders. One example of an Ethereum-based project is Rex MLS. This is an insurance platform that provides P2P access to all MLS information, including property listing and searching without the expense of hidden fees.

Identity and Privacy

Smart contracts will also be able to help streamline business processes by taking the place of traditional trust methods. Companies will be able to automate certain processes, like renewals, records release, and destruction. One project is called Trust Stamp and it uses data that is publicly available and social media to verify a user's identity, providing them with a unique trust score.

Another authentication and verification system is called Chainy, using timestamps to record things permanently onto the blockchain while Uport is an identity and key management system. Built with both developers and users in mind, it is made up of smart contracts and open-source libraries that allow used to own and control their identity, reputation, assets and online data.

Entertainment

The blockchain can mend issues with copyrights, tracking and payments, and there are several platforms already set up with the aim of decentralizing the music industry. They all make use of Ethereum and smart contracts to provide artists with complete control over their work by removing the likes of Spotify, SoundCloud and ReverbNation from the equation.

The gaming world has also expressed interest in Ethereum with several real-world games that provide users with a way of winning rewards. Gambling sites are jumping on the bandwagon, allowing users to deposit and claim their winnings in a fast and safe way. Not only will this cause disruption to the online gambling industry, it will also provide gamblers with safety and security from scams.

Lastly, there are the social media sites based on Ethereum, like Akasha. This site allows users to publish work, vote on other work and share it across the platform. It aims to be a decentralized version of WordPress but, unlike WordPress, Akasha provides rewards to those who come up with rich content though curator's rewards.

Smart Infrastructure

Ethereum has blasted into the smart infrastructure industry by facilitating the trading of, renting of and selling of energy and other peer-to-peer products. One Ethereum-based company called Slock.it is aiming to bring the blockchain and the Internet of Things together to help foster more P2P transactions. ElectricChain used Ethereum technology to hasten the speed at which solar energy takes off. They do this by going into partnership with other companies to provide incentives for the collection and use of solar energy.

LO3 Energy has just been awarded a patent that allows Ethereum-based energy trading. Together with Siemens, they came up with the Transactive Grid, a microgrid project in use in Brooklyn New York. The project is a P2P platform for energy trading that allows neighbors to buy and sell energy to and from each other.

The Health Industry

Ethereum has the potential to revolutionize health care systems across the world. Every hospital in the world will be able to store patient records, access them and share them when and where needed. This is one of the biggest factors in the development of new vaccinations for outbreaks of a viral nature or in the fight to prevent them from happening in the first place. You could, for example, go on holiday to Spain, pop in to see the doctor and then, when you return to Manhattan, where you live, go to see your doctor there and both will have access to the exact same information about you.

It doesn't end there though. The recent craze in wearables is picking up steam and they are not going anywhere. Smartwatches record health data that could be shared with every single hospital in the world, allowing medical condition patterns to be spotted, such as strokes or heart attacks and you could be given a warning before it happens. In short, Ethereum could save your life.

Simpler Transactions

Right now, the entire economy of the world is based on transactions of one kind or another and these are about to be changed for good by Ethereum. Smart contracts will make it easy to exchange anything that is of value without any risk to either party. Instead of coming up with an old-fashioned paper contract, the whole thing will be done in computer code. Say, for example, you wanted to buy a photograph. Now, you would purchase it through a company like Shutterstock but, with a smart contract, you could set up a contract directly with the photographer. This can be done because of the built in IFTTT logic in Ethereum – If This Then That. The contract would state that, once the payment has been placed into an escrow service, the photograph will be sent. It could also say that, if the photo isn't sent, the payment will be returned to you.

Privacy from Third Parties

How many of you are aware that major search engines collect personal information from you and then sell it on to advertisers? And from that, they make a profit of billions every single year. By using the blockchain technology that Ethereum is based on, we can stop this from happening. Well, we can't stop the search engines from doing it but the technology can be used to log every single time those search engines use your information and data and will make those logs available publicly, for everyone to see. That way, the larger corporations will need to be a good deal more careful with the way they handle and use personal data if they don't want any damage done to their brand image.

Politics

Most people register to vote when the time comes around in their country, be it for local or national elections. However, not everyone places their vote because of a fear that their vote will not be counted or it will be altered in some way to favor a particular party. With Ethereum, voting and election fraud would be impossible. Because no one person has control of the network, every vote would be logged exactly as it was placed and everyone would be able to see it – they just wouldn't know who placed it. And that publicity means that no vote could be altered without everyone knowing about it, leading to a much fairer and more democratic system everywhere.

Self-Driving Cars

Some time ago, search engine giant Google announced plans to start mass-production of self-driving cars in 2020, hoping to revolutionize the way transport systems work. Ethereum has a vested interest in this because it is their technology that will back these vehicles up.
Self-drive cars are safer too because each communicates with the rest and that communication happens way faster than you or I could ever comprehend, let alone actually try.

Data Storage

The likes of Microsoft and Dropbox use server farms to store vast amounts of data. A server farm is a building full of these servers, each one full of information but they have one inherent problem – the company that owns them tends to concentrate a large proportion of capacity in one location. That opens the company up to a terrorist attack, natural disaster or some other way in which data can be stolen, lost or destroyed, resulting in substantial losses.

Decentralized storage facilities are the solution, facilities where information is not stored in one place; it is stored on millions of computers spread across the world. So far, this hasn't been possible because to the huge challenge involved in building the networks that could connect every server in safety and with fast rates of data transfer. The solution is likely to be Ethereum because the blockchain technology is designed to encrypt information and transfer data very quickly between all the servers

Prediction: Blokchain Changing The World In Many Ways

Below are examples of how blockchain technology through the use of *Ethereum* applications will revolutionalized the world we live in for years to come!

Banks - Blockhain technology will enable almost everyone around the world, even people living in third world countries to have the means of financial access via bitcoin (BTC). -BTC uses fundamental blockchain technology to function.

Cyber Security - Although blockchain is accessible to the public it uses complex math and cryptography to enhance security, thus making it extremely difficult for anyone to hack and tamper with it.

Supply Chain Management - All transactions are permanently recorded in sequential order from point of begging to end, and constantly monitored through general consensus among the blockchain network for accuracy and authenticity purposes.- Increasing efficiency, reducing errors and time delays.

Insurance - Insurance is based on the principal of trust management, blockchain can be used to accurately verify data, such as insured person's identity, residence, etc. The chances for fraud is extremely slim as you know blockchain has state of the art advanced security measures.

Transportation - We've all heard of Uber? Well now blockchain is looking to create decentralized peer to peer ride sharing apps, ways for car owners and users to establish terms and conditions of transportation without third party intermediaries (Uber).

Charity - Common issues with charities are corruption and inefficiencies. Blockchain technology will ensure transparent record keeping and create a permanent sequential, tamper resistant record to track, so there are no chances of money scandals or frauds we always hear about in the news. Ensuring only the intended recipient receives the funds.

Voting - Voting scandals and rigging can happen anywhere in the world, and even here in the west we are not immune to scandals, remember the 2016 US election? It's not the first time political parties have been accused for rigging results. Blockchain technology can be utilized for voter registration and identity confirmation , and also electronic vote counting would ensure only legitimate votes are counted.

No votes could be taken away or added, thus creating an indisputable publically accessible ledger. How's that for democracy?

Governments - Government system are often slow, ambiguous and extremely frustrating. Implementing blockchain based systems will decrease bureaucracy, increase efficiency and uphold transparency.

Health Care - Secure storage platforms for information utilizing blockchain technology will enhance security and prevent hacking. Safely storing data such as medical records and sharing it only with the intended recipient. Improving data security and possibly even speed up diagnosis.

Energy Management - This has been a centralized monopoly for the longest time. But with blockchain technology you would be able to buy forms of energy, ie : electricity in a peer to peer fashion, thus electricity producers and users could buy directly from each other on a decentralized system. Currently we have to use trusted private intermediaries.

Online Music - Blockchain technology is working on a way to pay musicians and artists directly, instead of forfeiting large chunks of royalties to platforms or record labels. Artists/musicians would be able to keep more of the their profits!

Retail - Connecting buyers and sellers without additional fees. Exchanging in commerce without middlemen or intermediaries. In this case blockchain technology would use smart contract systems, and built in reputation management systems.

Real Estate - Eliminate the archaic paper based record keeping system, fraud, and uphold transparency. Blockchain would ensure ownership, accuracy, and even transferring property deeds.

Crowd Funding - A lot of companies use crowd funding platforms, however often times these platforms charge high fees. Blockchain could eliminate these fees by implementing smart contracts and online reputation based systems. New projects would release funds by generating their own "tokens" that have an associated value, and later be exchanged for products, services or cash.

Chapter 4: Investing in Ethereum

If you were looking to invest in an industry that shows a fast growth, there is a good chance that you would be looking at something in the tech sector or even marijuana stocks but, if you want something that has an accumulative return there your absolute best bet is Ethereum. Since 2017 started, despite a sudden drop in price, Ethereum's value has gone up by more than 2500% year to date. The S&P 500, by comparison, took almost 40 years to achieve those heady heights. There are a few ways to invest in Ethereum and we're going to talk about them here. Incidentally, one of the easiest ways is to purchase Bitcoin first and then use that to purchase Ether.

How Do I Buy Ether?

If you want to purchase Ether, the Ethereum currency, you will need to make use of an exchange. There are some exchanges that will store your keys for you, privately, and this makes it very easy to buy and sell but you do lose on the security aspect. There is also the issue of having a third-party looking after your information for you and that is not the idea of a decentralized system. If that exchange was hacked, and it has happened, your keys also get hacked and your access to your Ether is gone forever. The best alternative is to store your own keys offline or by using hardware – the most secure method but also the most difficult. You would need to be sure that your hardware never got corrupted or destroyed or you never lost the piece of paper that your keys get printed onto. Does it not also strike you as being just a little ironic that, to store your keys for a digital online currency, you need to use paper? More about storage later

What is an ICO?

An ICO is an Initial Coin Offering and it is a way of buying tokens in a specific company. In return, normally you will get some voting rights in the management of the company or, in some cases, a share of the profits. All of this is managed by way of the smart contracts we talked about earlier.

So how do you buy Ether?

The Easy Way – A Card Purchase

If this is your first time investing in a cryptocurrency, the best and easiest way is to go through CoinBase. They allow you to purchase and sell Ether using a credit card and they take away the need to get an exchange involved.

CoinBase is one of the best respected, the easiest to use and the most trustworthy way to purchase cryptocurrencies and they offer a decent desktop interface and a great mobile app. You can purchase any amount of Ether from $10 right up to $1000 in any coin. However, because they are one of the most popular, new registrations on CoinBase are reportedly being held up because of the increased demand, especially during peak times. These issues should be cleared fairly soon but, in the meantime, there are other ways to buy.

Cex.io

This is a full exchange, offering users the opportunity to purchase Ether using a credit card in USD, GBP or Euros. It is recommended that you sign up to both CoinBase and CEX as you will stand a chance of getting access when it is busy – especially if CoinBase goes down. This is one of the friendliest of all the main exchanges, offering a well-designed user-friendly interface.

BitPanda

BitPanda is primarily focused on the European market and is based in Austria. This exchange allows you to use SEPA, Skrill, and Visa to purchase Ether. Again, it has a very friendly user interface and also allows you, should you also purchase Bitcoins, to transfer them into vouchers for Amazon DE. This is a highly recommended exchange for anyone based in Austria or Germany.

Coinmama

Coinmama has only recently expanded into the Ether market and, right now you can only make your purchase using Euros or USD. However, they do accept all major credit

and debit cards for payment. The biggest benefit to using Coinmama is that, as soon as you have bought Ether, it is transferred directly to your wallet – more about those later

– as opposed to some exchanges that hold your coins. With Coinmama, you have total control and have the ability to direct them to your exchange address or you can transfer them into another type of altcoin.

The Slightly Harder Way – Through an Exchange

The exchanges in this section may take longer for you to understand how they work and how to navigate their user-interface. However, often the fees are much lower and you get more features to play with. If you are looking for a more serious investment option, these are the better ones to get involved with.

It is also worth noting that withdrawals and deposits to these exchanges tend to be easier and that is a critical point – when you make a purchase through an exchange unless you are intending to sell it immediately, remove it to a wallet. If you don't and the exchange gets hit by a hacker you may lose all your Ether in one fell swoop. There is also the chance of a service outage on any exchange.

The downside is that not all of them make it easy to pay using Euros, GBP or USD and you may incur quite high bank fees if they do. This is only cost effective if you are buying a decent amount but it is always worth checking because you may not always be able to pay by card.

One of the best recommendations is to register with several exchanges – you don't need to make a purchase on each of them right away. It can take several days for account verification to be completed so you need to have them ready in case you need access. Not only that, prices can vary from exchange to exchange and you want the best price you can possibly get.

The best full exchanges to look at are:

- Poloniex
- Kraken
- Gemini

Other Services

eToro

This is a social trading platform that makes decisions that are based on social investment. Your investment will be based on the collation of actions by many and it offers a nice simple interface to help you make your investment.

eToro allows you to trade on an ETH/USD exchange, most probably the easiest way to get some exposure to the currency without the need to go too much into technical set ups. It is regulated by the UK FCA and is thought to be one of the safest methods of trading across a wide variety of markets.

A Copy Fund has recently been introduced by eToro, allowing you easier exposure to digital currencies and this gives you an easier way of making a mainstream investment without the need to monitor and manage your coins yourself.

It is important for you to understand that you will not own the coins through eToro; instead, you are making an investment in a price-tracking fund so make sure you only invest an amount that you can comfortably afford to lose.

How to Store Your Ether

You have purchased your Ether so what do you do now? Leave it where it is? Hope that the value is going to shoot up? Certainly, there is every chance that can happen but, similarly, there is also every chance it could plummet and the worst thing you could do is leave your currency sitting on the exchange while you wait for it to go up again. Not every exchange is up and running all the time and the only time that you will be able to access your Ether is when it is. That restricts your access. One of the most common

reasons for a service to go down, particularly in the case of CoinBase, is high demand or server problems and these are common.

So, the best thing you can do is store your Ether in a wallet and these come in several formats:

- Digital – stored on your mobile device or computer
- Paper – an archived print of you details
- Hardware – USB sticks that retain your keys and can only be accessed through a code. This is the most secure method

There are lots of arguments that go in favor of or against these wallets and each has its own benefits. The most crucial factor is that you, and you alone, maintain sufficient security on your wallet to keep your coins safe. If you lose your information or your wallet is compromised, you could lose everything. These are the most common wallets used for the storage of Ether:

A word of warning first – never lose your wallet password. If you do or you can't remember it you cannot access your wallet and there is no way to reset your password.

- **Jaxx**

Jaxx will run on a mobile, a desktop, and a browser and has support for many altcoins, including Ether, Bitcoin and Litecoin. It is dead simple to set up and very easy to use.

- **Mist**

Mist wallet is linked directly to the official website for Ethereum but it is a little on the slow side and can be very technical, not always suited for beginners.

- **My Ether Wallet (MEW)**

MEW is by far the best and most popular of all the Ether wallets. You do not need to sign up for it and set up is dead simple. There is plenty of help available for inexperienced users and experienced ones. The wallet is based on a local storage system and the password is the single most important bit of information that you will have.

MEW also provides support for sending Ether using a hardware wallet or you can generate a paper wallet, keeping your currency offline completely.

Hardware Wallets

Hardware wallets are very high tech, long term and incredibly secure forms of storage. Prices start at about 80 euros for anything decent so if you don't intend to spend that much on your Ether investment it may not be worth using one. The two most popular hardware wallets are Trezor and Ledger Nano S. Both do have relatively long waiting lists though so if you really want one, get your name down and then use one of the other wallets while you wait – and be patient!

Who is investing in Ethereum?

Although Ethereum can be seen as the child of Bitcoin, when it comes to future promise, it has shot past its predecessor, leaving it in the dust. There is one thing that sets Ethereum and Bitcoin worlds apart and that is the support that the former is receiving from both the technological and financial communities. Companies are beginning to realize the sheer power that blockchain technology provides in terms of efficiency and security and they want in.

Microsoft and JP Morgan are just two huge names that have pledged to support Ethereum's development by forming the Enterprise Ethereum Alliance, the purpose of which is to make sure that Ethereum's potential is fully realized across all industries. Companies that have joined the Alliance are working hard to ensure that a standard and open-source version of the platform is created, providing a blueprint of sorts for all future adaptations. JP Morgan is also working on its own Ethereum-based system of seamless fund transfers between its own branches across the world.

Although there are no small number of organizations that have invested in the leverage of Ethereum to act as a base for all privatized versions, one day, the goal they wish to attain is that every institution's private network will connect to the global blockchain, establishing a brand-new benchmark for transactions of information.

Other companies that have invested in Ethereum include:

- KYC-Chain – providing businesses with a safe way to attract new customers, using simple processes of identification and Know-Your-Customer. Customers are encouraged to manage their identities themselves, and only to share what information is necessary as and when needed.

- Colony – leveraging the Ethereum blockchains to drive organizations that are decentralized. It removes the traditional hierarchy of the organization and puts in place a simpler management of the distributed workforce. People are encouraged to invest expertise, time, ideas and feedback for global Ethereum projects. Based on an assessment system, users are given Ether tokens as rewards for completing tasks.

To list every company that has invested in Ethereum would take forever; suffice it to say that these are the tip of a very large iceberg.

Chapter 5: How Mining Works

Cryptocurrency mining is incredibly intensive work in terms of the processing power and the time that it takes. It is the participation in the distributed consensus network with the miner being rewarded in Ether tokens for coming up with solutions to the increasingly difficult math problems. Mining is done by pairing mining applications up with specific computer hardware.

All cryptocurrency transaction information must be embedded into a data block, with each block being lined through hash functions to the next and the previous block, hence the name, blockchain. Each block must be analyzed quickly to make sure that the platform runs smoothly but the developers of the Ethereum blockchain cannot do this alone – this is where the miners come in.

Miners are investors that give time space on their computer and energy to sort the blocks. When they come up with the right hash to solve the block, they submit their solution to the issues. Once it has been verified, the miner is given a reward, made up of a portion of the transaction they verified along with digital coins. The result of this is the Proof-of-Work system although Ethereum is switching over to a Proof of Stake System.

The only way, like Bitcoin, that Ethereum can be produced or created is through mining. However, with Ethereum, mining is doing more than just increasing the number of Ether in circulation – it is also used to secure the network as it works on the blocks in the blockchain. This process is essential to Ethereum because Ether is the fuel that keeps the platform running smoothly. One way of looking at it is that is a kind of incentive for developers to come up with fantastic applications. The supply of Ether is not infinite. Although there is no hard cap on it, it is limited to 25% of the initial issue at the presale, around 18 million Ether, every year.

For each block of Ether transactions to be validated in consensus, it must have the proof of work that proves the difficulty of it. Esthash is the name of the validation algorithm used and it is based on identification of the nonce input compared to the result in a way that it is lower than the initial threshold that was determined by the difficulty level. If all the outputs are uniformly distributed, the rewards are distributed on the time taken to find the nonce and that will depend on the difficulty of the block. In a case such as this, a miner can control the time needed to find the new bloc by manipulating the difficulty level.

Unlike Bitcoin, which is now too expensive and difficult, Ether can comfortably be mined from your own home. You will need to have knowledge of script writing and of the command prompt but it is relatively easy and very exciting once the process has been broken down into more manageable steps. Before you learn those steps, you need to understand the basics behind Ethereum mining.

The Basics

The first thing you need to understand is that mining takes a lot of power. However, provided your mining is done efficiently, you can generate income through the sale of the Ether. You can download a mining calculator from the internet which will give you some idea of what your profit will be.

You can use your home computer for Ethereum mining, unlike Bitcoin that requires expensive specialized hardware. The only caveats are that your graphic card must be a good one with a minimum of 2 GB RAM. Forget about CPU mining; it will just leave you frustrated, so much so that we are not even going to discuss it. GPU mining is far more efficient and at least 200 times faster than CPUs for mining purposes. If you have a Nvidia card, consider swapping it out for a decent AMD card as they are much better. You will also need at least 30 GB of free space on your computer – this is for the software you will need and to store the blockchain. Don't forget, the blockchain is constantly growing with each transaction that is added to it and if you can't store it, you can't mine.

The Procedure for Ethereum Mining

Follow these steps exactly for true mining success:

Step 1 - Download Geth. This is an application that serves as the communication hub, providing you with a link to the Ethereum platform while, at the same time, ensuring your setup is coordinated – that includes all your hardware and software. Geth will also provide you with reports on a development that you need to take action on.

Step 2 – Because Geth is in zipped file format, you will need to unzip it and extract the contents. Then you can transfer the Geth file to your hard drive. Most people stick to using C: but you can use a partition on your drive if you want.

Step 3 – To execute the application, you will need to use the command prompt. If you are using Windows, simply click on the search bar and type in CMD. Click on Command Prompt from the list of results.

Step 4 – The username placeholder on your computer is C:\Users\Username> and this provides the name given to your computer. It is the display that you will usually see in the command terminal. Your next step is to find Geth s, at the command prompt, type in cd/ and press the Enter button on your keyboard. This is a command that changes the directory and you should now see highlighted on the screen C:\> You are now in the C: drive.

Step 5 – Next comes account creation. To call Geth, at the command prompt, type in geth account new and press enter. You should now see C:\>geth account new at the command prompt.

Step 6 – Now you need to set up a password. Take care over this; make it a strong password and type it in carefully – you must remember this password! Press enter and your account with geth has been created.

Step 7 – Before you can do anything geth must link up to the network so, at the command prompt, type in geth -rpc and press enter. The Ethereum blockchain will begin to download and will synchronize with the global network. This is not a quick job and much will depend on how large the blockchain is and your computer and network speed. Do not do anything else until this step is complete.

Step 8 – Next, you must download the mining software. This will help your GPU to run the necessary hash algorithm. One of the better choices is Ethminer so find it on the internet and download it, then install it on your computer.

Step 9: Now change your directory again at the command prompt – see step 4 for instructions. Open a new command terminal by right-clicking the open one and selecting terminal from the popup menu

Step 10 – In this new window, type in cd prog and then press the tab key. You should now see C:\>cd prog on your terminal screen. Press the tab key again and you will see C:\> cd "Program Files:' press the enter key again and you will see displayed C:\Program Files>

Step 11 – To get into the mining software folder, at the prompt, type in cd cpp and the press the tab key and the enter key. Press the tab key again and you should see C:\Prgram Files\cpp-ethereum on the display

Step 12 – To begin GPU mining, type in ethminer -G and press the enter key. The mining process will begin after the Directed Acrylic Graph (DAG) is built. This is a very large file that is stored on your GPU RAM for making it ASIC resistant. ASIC stands for Application Specific Integrated Circuits. Do make sure you have enough space on your hard drive before you do this.

Step 13 – If you want to, at this stage, you could have a go at CPU mining. All you need to do is type ETHMINER at the command prompt and then press the enter key. Again, the DAG will need to be built, after which Geth will begin communicating with Ethminer.

The Future of Ethereum Mining

Right now, Ethereum is using a Proof-Of-Work algorithm, the backbone of Bitcoin mining. Proof-of-Work is referring to finding solutions to complicated math equations, a fundamental requirement for any miner to get their block added to the blockchain. However, because of the sheer amount of energy it takes, this system has been pulled apart and Ethereum came up with another way. Using the Dagger Hashimoto algorithm, they have found a way that allows the home computer to mine relatively easily, without the added cost.

Also, they are planning to replace this system with a Proof of Stake System. This will remove the whole concept of mining and the new system will be powered by a consensus algorithm. Because the network is a string of computer-maintained connections, the profit that can be gained from mining Ether is somewhat surreal. Many miners are of the opinion that mining will come to a stop altogether when the new system comes into place – whether it will or not, only time will tell.

Chapter 6: What Does the Future Hold for Ethereum?

Right now, Ethereum is in an interesting place. Having fought through several battles, such as the DAO attack and the hard fork that followed, it has come through relatively unscathed. Now, it can expand and become what it was intended to be – a truly unique platform that is set to cause a huge disruption in industries the world over.

Ethereum is undergoing constant development and change and one of the biggest changes to date is the change over from Proof-of-Work to Proof-of-Stake. This is going to turn mining into a virtual process; instead of miners, there will be validators, who will be required to provide a certain amount of their Ether as a stake. Blocks are validated through the placement of a bet and the reward you get if the block is placed is in proportion to your initial investment. If your bet goes on a malicious block or the wrong block, you lose your Ether.

The advantages of this system are what will shape the future of the Ethereum platform:

- Lower costs in terms of energy and money – right now, Bitcoin miners are spending an average of $50,000 per hour on energy - $1.2 million every day. The proof-of-stake algorithm will cut these costs off almost completely because it will be a virtual system
- No advantage for ASIC hardware – there will be no advantages for those who have better hardware because the system won't depend on it
- 52% attacks will be harder – these happen when one person or a group has more than 50% of the hashing power in their control. Proof-of-stake will negate this.
- No malicious validators – because validators have to lock up a certain amount of their own Ether in the blockchain they are not likely to add any malicious or wrong blocks – they would lose their stake
- Faster block creation – the entire process of creating the new blocks will become more efficient and faster

This will also ensure the blockchain is more scalable because it will be much faster and easier to check who has invested the biggest stake than it is to see who has the highest amount of hashing power. Coming to a consensus will be simpler and more efficient.

The Future of Proof-of-Stake

At this moment, Casper, the POS algorithm is getting ready to be implemented. To begin with, mining will continue as normal but every 100th block will be subject to a POS check. Eventually, most of the block creation process will move over to POS and the way they are going to do it is through an ice age. What this means is that mining will become much harder and this will cut the hash rate. In turn, this will cut the speed of the chain and the decentralized applications that run on it, thus forcing everyone onto the POS system.

This is not going to be hassle-free. One massive fear is that the miners may force a hard fork in the blockchain before this can happen and then carry on with the new chain, mining as they always have done. Considering we already had one hard fork, this could potentially mean three blockchains running side by side.

Right now, this is nothing more than speculation. Before we get that far, there are two more phases of Ethereum implantation to go, the phases are:

- Frontier – the version everyone got when they started
- Homestead – the current phase
- Metropolis – the next phase
- Serenity – the final phase

Metropolis is being implemented but before we can even begin to look at it, there are three terms that you need to become au fait with:

- Abstraction
- Zk-snarks
- Sharding

Abstraction

What this means is that any protocol or system can be used by anyone without a need to know all the ins and outs, all the technical details that go with it. For example, you don't need to be an engineer to use an iPhone; you just need to know what buttons to press. You don't need to know about the circuits that are activated when you tap on an app or even how that app was programmed.

Zk-Snarks

This stands for Zero-Knowledge Succinct Non-Interactive Argument of Knowledge. The system has its base in zero knowledge proofs and that works something like this – you have two separate parties – a prover and a verifier. The prover is able to prove to the verifier that they know a certain piece of information without actually revealing that information, thus aiding in privacy.

Sharding

Sharding means nothing more than breaking a massive database down into smaller shards. Each shard will have its own validators and this will help with scalability.

Metropolis

There are 4 main implementations in the Metropolis Phase:

- Implementation of several Ethereum Improvement Protocols – EIPs, which will work to make the Ethereum platform more robust
- Flexibility for smart contracts. They will have the ability to pay their fees without the need for external funding from users
- The first steps to abstraction – to make Ethereum more user-friendly to the masses. One possible innovation may be that users will be allowed to pay their Ethereum transaction costs using another cryptocurrency other than Ether
- Zk-Snarks will be introduced

Serenity

Although the implementation of Serenity is some way off, it will be the final one, Ethereum as it should be. When Serenity is finally launched, this will be the result:

- More EIPS will be implemented
- Proof-of-Work will be gone and will be entirely replaced by Proof-of-Stake
- A total abstraction of the Ethereum platform
- Blockchain sharding will be implemented. This will ensure that the blockchain, all transactions, and all the decentralized applications that run on Ethereum will be able to run a great deal faster and block creation times will decrease exponentially. It is expected that the times will drop to below 4 seconds per block – compare that to the 10 to 20 minutes that Bitcoin blocks currently take.

The Future of Ethereum

With all of this, there is no doubt that Ethereum has an incredibly bright future. Ultimately, Ethereum has one aim – to "disappear" although not literally. The ultimate goal is for Ethereum to become omnipresent, running on everything without everyone being aware that they are working on or using an Ethereum-based system.

Summary

Ethereum is the digital oil and framework. Ethereum has several applications and is very versatile. Unlike bitcoin which is only really used as a form of currency in commerce. The best way to comprehend what Ethereum is to use an anaology, earlier I called Ethereum a digital oil and similar to petroleum it has various functions and uses. While bitcoins can be considered a one dimensional property that can only be used for one thing and that is a form of currency.

Remember in essence Ethereum is basically a blockchain technology, however, the main difference is with Ethereum you can actually build things, ie: bitcoins and other cryptocurrencies, additionally you can also build social networks, and decentralized information sources similar to wikipedia. The programming language in Ethereum is like Java or CC+, meaning you can build almost anything!

So for example, if you wanted to build the next "Facebook" or another social media platform using Ethereum it would be completely decentralized! That means there would be no third party intermediaries, no incorporation and no authoritative figure. Therefore, all users would be communicating directly, peer to peer, and all the data and information collected would belong to the users and not anyone else!

So think how this would translate into add campaigns and the such? Users would be directly paid, instead of money being funneled through third party intermediaries who take a cut or hold on to the funds. Incredibly enough this actually equates to you being a "shareholder" of the network technically speaking. Exciting right?

So whatever network or application you are engaging with, you'd automatically become a shareholder! Imagine a new application or platform just launched, and in order to utilize their services they hand out tokens as a means of purchasing services. Now if the application becomes popular and more people join all the first time user's tokens would rise in value as now there would be a demand for them, and thus creates a sort of shareholder paradigm.

In essence Ethereum is a platform for decentralized applications. The future looks bright for Ethereum, more and more people in society are realizing the true value this technology can bring. Microsoft and other giant corporations are heavily investing in Ethereum as we speak. The potential is recognized and the future seems boundless. It's really important to understand the power of this amazing technology and it will transform the way the internet works. The basic architecture for the internet as we have it now is clients need to go through servers, for instance when I go to Facebook my browser is the client and needs to connect to the central Facebook server, and then all the communication goes through the centralized server. But, with a decentralized social network server all my messages will be sent directly to the users whom I want to talk with and not a central server.

This is incredible for the future! This could mean we could literally be reengineering the way communication occurs in cyberspace. What are your thoughts on Ethereum? Will this technology revolutionize the world? Only time will tell.

Bonus Chapters

Bitcoin Expanded

Although the history of BTC is somewhat obscure the estranged man behind both the development of BTC and the initial stages of blockchain is Satoshi Nakamoto. This all started approximately in the year 2008. It is believed Mr. Nakamoto posses **1 million** BTC that have a cash value of **2.7 billion USD**!! (Present year 2017)

The group of people who assisted in the development of BTCs is still an enigma and there is a lot of mystery that shrouds this question even today, however we do know for certain that Mr. Nakamoto and his group of developers intended to have some sort of new electronic cash system implemented during economic crisis between the years 2007 - 2008. This was an extremely strategic and clever ploy trying to leverage the world's economic turmoil and capitalize on it by introducing a totally radical, new, unparalleled, and revolutionary currency.

This cryptocurrency would be the first ever intangible form of money that only exists in "cyberspace". BTC has its limits, and by that I mean it is a finite currency and capped at a maximum threshold of 21 million to be brought into existence. Meaning once that cap is reached no more BTC can ever be produced.

There is a lot of controversy surrounding the true identity of Mr. Satoshi Nakamoto or if this is even a real person. There are a lot of speculations ranging from being someone from "common wealth origins" to being a Japanese - American born systems engineer, I cannot give a definitive answer to this conjecture. But, what I can say is ever since the debut of BTC it has been continuously gaining upward momentum and shows no signs of slowing down and is currently worth *2739.26 USD* per BTC! That's right, $2739 USD for a single bitcoin! (current value estimated **July 2017**)

Obviously just like any market share value will fluctuate due to various factors in the free market. Therefore, you can expect big spikes and deep declines, but I can say BTC is most definitely a lucrative prospect and something worthwhile investing in. It is a currency that is here to stay for the foreseeable future and will continue to impact the lives of millions of people worldwide.

BTC has made more than a handful of people millionaires, including myself. How was this done? Simply put I zoned in on an opportunity, saw a trend and predicted the future based on past patterns. Not difficult at all right? Perhaps I used a bit of "chance" too, I was in the right place at the right time. In all honesty, when it comes to capitalizing on trends you must be able to discern, time, and take massive action towards it, and then you will be rewarded with fruition from the risk you took. Before BTC gained its high value, when youtube videos, blogs on BTC, and "How to do" books /articles weren't around, BTC's value was worth less than a fraction of its value today.

Me and many others purchased BTC when they were priced around $14 -$35 USD per BTC. As you can see the price has exponentially increased and those who invested early as always reap massive results! Now you're probably questioning is it too late to join in on the "BTC gold rush"? My answer is, NO. There is still a massive opportunity that exists to make a killing and capitalize on this BTC trend.

Historical Trends

Since the history of mankind technological advancements that spurred waves of monumental change shaped the world in which we live today, such as the renaissance, industrial age, etc. At any given period of time in history we see patterns, trends and paradigms that shape the world we live in today.

BTC will be the next BIG trend and will shift government policies, regulations, and legislation forever. Imagine a decentralized system with no authoritative institutions s in control, no detrimental government intervention, but only the will of the people manifested through an autonomous currency. Isn't this incredible?

Of course people will be skeptical at first, but as we look at history's historical trend we can see anytime massive change or revolution occurs it was always met with opposition, consisting of people who are skeptic about change. Anytime new knowledge or technology was implemented it was always mocked, ridiculed and even denied.

Please see below an excerpt from the book Blockchain Technology & Blueprint Ultimate Guide. You can see recent historical events that occurred that continue to change the world for the better in which we live today..

"We live in the digital age and it would only make sense that currency would eventually follow in the transition into the digital realm, ie: cryptocurrency. This is not merely speculation or abstract conjecture, but this is based on trends and a few facts. Let's take a look at some of the things we interface with on a daily basis that have also stepped into the world digitization."

Books - In the past libraries were the only source to get access to books and other information packages. But, now we have digital books (kindle, Kobo,etc).

Music/Podcasts - Before you had to buy records, tapes, and CDs to listen to your favorite artist. Now we have itunes and other platforms that allow you to instantly listen to music without having to go through the hassle of buying an actual physical product. Digital access to music eliminates the damaged merchandise factor, for example a scratch on a CD would render the music on it inaudible, meaning you would have to go buy another copy! With music being digital you eliminate such inconveniences.

Video Games - Synonymous to music this too has stepped into the digital era. Games use to be purchased on cartridges and most recently CDs, but now can all be downloaded at the touch of a button online for instant access.

Mail - Before the invention of the E-mail the vast majority of people in society solely relied on mail couriers (mail men/women) as a means of relaying communication. However, since the advent and successful launch of the E-mail people now communicate worldwide with lightning speed! Uninterrupted by time zones and other external factors.

Bill Payments - In the past the average person had to rely on cheques to get paid and to exchange large volumes of cash in any given transaction. Bills would have to be paid by cheque, and the period of waiting times were immensely long. But, now we have direct deposits (Electronic Wire Transfers) and other similar electronic deposits. We can even make bill   payments and purchases directly from our smart phones!

As you can see the above historical trends, some more recent than others indicates quite a few things, 1. accessibility and autonomy is an increasing trend, and 2. Evolution is an inevitable variable and we must adapt accordingly. It's only a matter of time when currency also follows in the digital paradigm. After all this is the digital age, right?

Advantages:

Decentralized system - Nobody has ownership, no authoritative institutions have control, and governments cannot intervene.

Utilizes BlockChain technology - Because BTC uses blockchain technology it makes this cryptocurrency tamper resistant and extremely difficult for fraud and any other shady transactions unlikely.

Hyper Ledger - utilizes a ledger that records every single transaction that occurs. Which can be used to trace transaction with pinpoint accuracy from point of origin to finish.

Finite Currency - BTC is a finite currency and has a cap. Meaning unlike banks, you cannot print out new money on demand. (this is what causes inflation - money loses value)

Accounts Cannot Be Frozen - It's a known fact that banks for whatever reasons, when they become suspicious of certain financial activity they have the right to either freeze your account or terminate it without any warning or legitimate reason. Don't believe me? Read the fine print the next time you sign up with whomever you decide bank with.

This has actually happened to a friend of mine before, he use to operate an event management company which was quite lucrative, and one time he was expecting a deposit of **250,000 USD** and even advised the branch manager at the time, but can you guess what happened? For whatever reason they still decided to flag his personal bank account and it was frozen for "further investigation" and there was absolutely nothing he could do about it.

He ran a legitimate business, and fortunately he did eventually get access to his bank account 2 weeks later, however imagine the amount stress and headaches he had to go through. He had to pay vendors, employees, and other expenses, yet he could not touch any of his money that he rightfully owned.

But with BTC accounts cannot be frozen. So if the same scenario went down with depositing BTC he would of had no hassle or any problems whatsoever.

No Prerequisites - Laws and regulations vary from country to country, however the fact is that banks have limits and arbitrary rules to control your money. With BTC all you.

Direct Person To Person Transfer- With BTC there are no intermediaries, clearing houses or middlemen you find with traditional banks. I personally like this approach a lot better as large volume transactions can be done with ease, fluidly and efficiently with no long waiting times. Money can be received instantly.

Transaction Fees Significantly Decreased - Let's face it banks are not looking for the best interest of the people. Expensive transaction and hidden fees is something we are all constantly bombarded with, and can be costly. But with BTC you will face significantly reduced fees compared to banks.

Disadvantages

No customer technical or customer support - Since BTC runs on a decentralized system, when you run into trouble perhaps your hard drives crashes, you lost your password or unique key code, the fact is you have nobody to turn to. Banks would have customer support.

Bitcoin Value Volatile - Simply put the value of BTC can be erratic, and if someone hypothetically came up with a better cryptocurrency with a greater algorithm what happens to BTC? The value would surely drop, and thus BTC can be considered unstable for this reason.

Negative perceptions - Ever since the rise of "silk road" a black market website selling illegal goods in exchange for BTC, bitcoins got quite a bad rep due to the fact it was used as a veil for criminals to conduct commerce under.

Banks Do Not Support Bitcoin - The fact is BTC threatens the very existence of financial institutions and they do not at all like the fact that BTC a decentralized system and currency exists. Banks have terminated many accounts of users who engaged in mixing BTC with their bank accounts.

No Physical Properties - BTC in reality has no actual value, but just like any fiat currency it is given value by us. Remember BTC is intangible, it's not like gold, silver or copper.

BTC is an electronic currency that is based on a unified maintained ledger. People transfer "bitcoin currency" by sending messages to the bitcoin network known as maintainers or "miners" who verify signatures in the form of complex math equations. Maintainers/miner do a general consensus to find out the accurate solution and verify the authenticity of the message from the account holder.

BTC in actual fact has no value, but achieves its value because we give it value just like any other fiat currency. BTC is a completely intangible substance unlike the physical currency we use today.

We must highlight an important aspect of BTC, and that's what happens if user error mistakes are made, such as hard drive crashes which stores your pertinent "key code information"? This will result in a permanent loss of BTC associated with the account holder's private key code.

Since its a decentralized system there is no technical support or bank teller assistance you can turn to, thus your BTCs are lost forever.

Conclusion

I want to thank you for taking the time to read my guide. I hope that you now have a better understanding of what Ethereum is all about and how you can make a profit from it by investing or mining.

Despite the fact that it is still not close to the value of Bitcoin, Ether has been on an impressive growth spurt just recently. Since it made its debut on the eToro platform in January 2017, impressive and incredibly gains have been registered, its value quadrupling almost overnight. Of course, some of that could be down to a decision made recently by the SEC to deny a Bitcoin-based ETF, perhaps causing some investors to turn to Ether instead.

Ether is a new currency, just a couple of years old and it still depends quite a lot on the sentiment that cryptocurrencies seem to generate, although this is dictated mostly by Bitcoin. The original cryptocurrency is firmly established as an asset for a large number of traders, especially with the large swings it presents almost daily. Bitcoin has also been showing impressive gains but, in terms of the future, Ethereum is fast catching up and is ready to take over.

Bitcoin may still be the benchmark for overall market sentiment but the recent decision from the SEC has pushed it away from the mainstream market and this could well be why Ether is now surging in value. It isn't that far out to assume that many traders in cryptocurrencies are now turning to Ether as a viable alternative and especially as it hasn't yet had to face this kind of media trial.

Not only that, Ether is firmly established in its own right and is prone to upset by factors that do not have anything to do with Bitcoin. Because Ether is based on the blockchain, there are several development tools that could use Ether as their currency and that means any change in the Ethereum platform could influence the currency.

Whenever a hard fork is reached, a programming change that makes the platform backwards incompatible, Ether may well be severely affected – these could be positive, perhaps better security or better accessibility, or they could be negative as in the case of the DAO hard fork, an act that left the door open for the theft of $50 million in Ether, effecting a 30% value drop in 24 hours. That hack has been sorted and the value has begun climbing steadily again.

We can't yet determine whether Ethereum is going to be the next Bitcoin but we do expect to see a sizeable fluctuation in Ether prices as the future unfolds. It has the potential to carry on climbing becoming a very serious rival to Bitcoin or it could plummet hard, leading to its eventual demise. If the price of Bitcoin drops substantially, it can also take Ethereum down with it.

That said, Bitcoin has done a lot of work in paving the way for Ethereum. The market is now more tolerant and accepts digital currencies. This could be the start of a new era in money and finance, a new era where the strongest currencies are digital.

Ethereum is an interesting prospect and is one to watch now and in the future. Do be aware of the risks of investing though – it carries the same risks that any investment does so never invest any more than you can afford to lose.

If you enjoyed this book could you please leave a quality review on Amazon? See link below..

LINK: http://amzn.to/2uuGVt9

See Other Recommended books written By Raymond Kazuya

Blockchain Technology & Blueprint Ultimate Guide

LINK: http://amzn.to/2sQKeyM

Bitcoin & Cryptocurrencies Guide: Introduction Learn Everything You Need To Know!

LINK: : http://amzn.to/2tRQpyj

www.ingramcontent.com/pod-product-compliance
Lightning Source LLC
Chambersburg PA
CBHW052146070326
40689CB00050B/2174